MW00654310

WHY
GOD
WHY?

Praise for WHY, GOD, WHY?

"Not many religious thinkers deal with the greatest intellectual and emotional obstacle to religious faith—the unjust suffering that so many people experience. And even fewer deal with this subject as honestly, persuasively, and helpfully as Gershon Schusterman. Whatever your religion, or even if you identify with no religion, it is hard for me to imagine a person who would not find some—and quite possibly much—comfort from *Why, God, Why?* It is a great achievement."

—Dennis Prager is a nationally syndicated radio talk show host, Cofounder of PragerU, and author of The Rational Bible.

"Every person of faith must confront the question, why do the righteous often suffer while the wicked prosper? Rabbi Schusterman brings not only his vast experience and learning as a Torah scholar to provide an answer, but also his own devastating loss. With empathy, enthusiasm, and a profoundly engaging approach to such a difficult subject, the good rabbi offers a tract for the ages. Read this book!"

—Salvador Litvak, writer, director, Accidental Talmudist

"At last, a truly Jewish answer to pain and suffering that frames the subject with meaning, creating a path to resolution and comfort."

—Lori Palatnik, author and founding director, MomentumUnlimited.org

"For anyone who has suffered tragedy and wondered how God allowed it to happen, Rabbi Gershon Schusterman offers this sensitive, insightful, and hopeful book. Based on his own personal experience, he delves into timeless Jewish wisdom and shares reassuring answers to the question of 'Why do bad things happen to good people?' Rabbi Schusterman's book will help enable people who suffer tragedy to survive and hopefully thrive."

—Joseph Lieberman, former US Senator and Democratic vice-presidential nominee

"This book is a journey into the most heartrending question of all, the one that stuns us each time anew. It has grown out of personal loss and grief, yet also with conviction and resoluteness borne of faith. It will challenge you, expand your horizons, and stimulate your mind and heart."

—Rabbi YY Jacobson, internationally renowned Jewish lecturer and teacher, and dean of TheYeshiva.net

"Rabbi Schusterman proves that he is a leading, powerful, and gentle teacher of the human condition. His teachings are not only for the Jewish world but are relatable to people of all faiths everywhere. Through his story, we understand that though we cannot choose what life brings us, we can choose how to find peace and meaning in what has occurred. I hope I never "need" to use this book, yet if I do, it is a great comfort to know that it has been written."

—Gary Wexler, former professor at the USC Annenberg School of Communication, and advertising executive who directed campaigns for Fortune 100 clients

"The question of how a God of kindness, compassion, and fairness can allow and enable suffering and loss is the most difficult issue in Judaism—indeed, in any ethically based religious system. Moses struggled to understand it, Job and his friends fiercely debated it, but none of us has a complete answer. Rabbi Gershon Schusterman offers us a perspective that sheds light into a dark and frightening corner of reality. His valuable insights emerge from his impeccable Torah scholarship and from the agonizing crucible of personal experience with deep tragedy. His credibility to address these sensitive issues will not only impart understanding but also provide solace, comfort, courage and resilience. We owe him a debt of gratitude."

—Yitzchak A. Breitowitz, Rav, Kehillat Ohr Somayach, Jerusalem, Israel

RABBI GERSHON SCHUSTERMAN

WHY GOD WHY?

HOW TO BELIEVE IN HEAVEN
WHEN IT HURTS LIKE HELL

providence press
Los Angeles, California

WHY GOD WHY?

The author gratefully acknowledges the following: Andrews McMeel Syndication, for permission to quote from As seen in DEAR ABBY by Abigail Van Buren a.k.a. Jeanne Phillips and founded by her mother Pauline Phillips. © Andrews Mcmeel Syndication.   Jewish Educational Media, for permission to quote from *Brigadier General Ron Ronen-Pekker*, from the collection *My Story* (Vol. 1) © 2017.   Chabad. org, for permission to quote from Rabbi Aron Moss' article, *Why Do Bad Things Happen to Good People?* and from Rabbi Tzvi Freeman's article *Heresy in God's Name*.   The Rabbi Sacks Legacy Trust, for permission to quote from Rabbi Lord Jonathan Sacks and the footnote biography of Rabbi Sacks.   Little, Brown and Company, for permission to quote from *This Is My God* by Herman Wouk © 1988. The Orthodox Union's *Jewish Action* magazine, for permission to quote from Rabbi Zev Schostak's articles *Holding On or Letting Go: Reflections on Hospice in the Jewish Tradition* and *Final Confessions: Dialogues in a Jewish Geriatric Center*. © 2009, 1993.   Dow Jones & Company, for permission to quote from *The Wall Street Journal*'s op-ed "Before I Die," by Edmund N. Carpenter © 2010.   CIS Books, for permission to quote from Rabbi Dr. Abraham J. Twerski's *Let Us Make Man* © 1987. The Rabbinical Council of America, for permission to quote from Rabbi Norman Lamm's *The Face of God: Thoughts on the Holocaust*, in the book *Theological and Halakhic Reflections on the Holocaust* © 1992.   Shalem Press, for permission to quote from Eliezer Berkovits' book *God, Man and History* © 2004.   Sichos in English, for permission to quote from Rabbi Dovid Shraga Polter's book, *Chassidic Soul Remedies* © 2004.   Rohr Jewish Learning Institute, for permission to reprint the biography paragraphs appearing in footnotes throughout this book.   Material quoted from *Sefer Hasichos, 5688–5691; Kayitz 5700; Igrot Kodesh of Rabbi Joseph Isaac Schneersohn, vol. 8; Sefer Hasichos 5751; Likkutei Dibburim, Vol. I*, are © Kehot Publication Society and is printed here with permission.

ISBN: 978-0-8266-0832-1

Events described in this book are based on actual situations, but names and certain identifying details may have been changed.

The book's website is:
www.whygodwhythebook.com

Available at: **Kehot Publication Society Order Department:**
291 Kingston Avenue, Brooklyn, NY 11213
718-778-0226 / www.kehot.com

Printed in Türkiye

This book is dedicated to my family
who accompanied me on this journey

⁓

To my dear wife, Chana Rachel, who supported me
and who raised our children with loving dedication

⁓

To our cherished children
Sholom Yeshia, Eliyahu, Mendel,
Nechemia, Hinda, Ezzy, Berel,
Shula, Sheina, Kushi, and Tzippy

⁓

And to the blessed memory of their beloved mother,
Rochel Leah bat Sholom Yeshaya

Contents

Foreword by Rabbi Manis Friedman

Introduction	The Death of the Rabbi's Wife	1
Chapter 1	God's Defense Attorney	7
Chapter 2	The Challenge of Living With Evil	29
Chapter 3	What Is Evil, and Why Does It Exist?	45
Chapter 4	Is There Really a God?	65
Chapter 5	Is It Okay to Be Angry With God?	93
Chapter 6	Can Tragedy Refine Us?	121
Chapter 7	Is Suffering a Test of Faith?	141
Chapter 8	The Holocaust	169
Chapter 9	The Afterlife: Heaven, Hell, and Seeing the Light	195
Chapter 10	What If There Is No Explanation? How Do We Reach a Place of Peace?	219
Afterword	Adversity Doesn't Define Us How We Respond to It Does	251
Acknowledgments		257

Foreword

As students in *yeshivah* back in the early '60s, my friend Gershon Schusterman and I often found ourselves hotly discussing current issues, including those written about in the *Jewish Press*, a weekly newspaper. Despite our youth, we both enjoyed talking and debating the "bigger" issues of life. I recall one time when Gershon and I were deconstructing one article in particular that we agreed had treated a serious topic insensitively and with surprising shallowness—at least, that is how it appeared to our young minds.

I was quite content to simply share my opinions with my friend and then move on to other matters. Not Gershon. In the following week's newspaper, there was a letter to the editor addressing the article we had both found unsettling. The letter was articulate, nuanced, and well written, expressing a thoughtful, alternative approach to the issue. The author of the letter, as you no doubt have guessed, was my friend Gershon Schusterman. Even as a teenager, he already had the wisdom, the knowledge, the words, and the pen that could enlighten hearts and minds.

I'm pleased to say that Rabbi Schusterman and I have remained friends in the years of *yeshivah* and the many decades that have followed. Therefore, it came as no surprise that he has written such a deeply moving and important book about dealing with traumatic loss. In addition to all the wisdom and knowledge he has gained though his career as a rabbi, educator, and teacher, he has personally "walked the walk" and earned the right to "talk the talk." Unquestionably, this book will be invaluable to anyone coping with grief and loss, showing a pathway out of that darkness and back into the light.

Grief and sadness may seem like similar emotions, but they are not. A sad person wants to sleep; a grieving person cannot sleep. This is so because sadness is without life's vitality or energy, while grief is painfully alive with intense feeling. The two must not be conflated. When the grieving person is exhausted by the intensity of his grief, moving into a state of sadness may bring a measure of relief or escape. For others, the prospect of overwhelming emotion is so intimidating that they choose sadness (perhaps subconsciously) as an alternative response that lets them shut down all feelings.

These are instinctive and intuitive responses to painful and traumatic situations. But there is a third way, a path for us to find responsible, mindful, and reasoned answers that will allow us to ease our way through grief as time works its magic healing to our broken hearts.

The most troubling aspect of a trauma is the apparent senselessness of the event. It may be our essential humanity that bristles at an experience that seems pointless, mindless, and random. Our human intelligence seeks purpose, intention, and reason. Randomness offends the mind. Meaninglessness pains the soul.

The mature mind allows one to grieve deeply yet not become a "griever." In this evolved emotional state, we can understand grief as the acknowledgement of a loss of something precious: the more precious, the more the grief. Grieving is never an alternative to life but a painful regret at the loss of life. In this way, grief itself becomes an affirmation of life and of life's infinite value. Slowly, our grief goes through stages, moving the mind and heart back from the deep valley of loss to a gently sloping rise back to the joys of life, and from a terrible end to a new and improved beginning.

This transition is only possible when we can find meaning in our loss. Finding meaning calms the mind just as believing in its Divine purpose soothes the soul. When addressing the brokenhearted one must have the knowledge and wisdom of a sage and the sensitivity of an empathetic heart. Rabbi Gershon Schusterman has both qualities, which are on full display in this impressive and invaluable book.

Rabbi Manis Friedman

Rabbi Manis Friedman is the most popular rabbi on YouTube and author of Creating a Life That Matters.

The Death of the Rabbi's Wife

This is a book for the brokenhearted.

If you are going through a brutal, inexplicable loss—the death of a loved one, a shocking, unaccountable illness, a financial reversal, or any form of tragedy—I wrote this book for you.

In fact, if you are like me, you have quite possibly experienced a second loss that followed the first—a challenge to your faith, or perhaps even a loss of faith.

Isn't it God's job to keep us safe? Isn't it God's job to protect us, to love us, and to shield us from harm?

If so, when tragedy strikes, where are we supposed to turn? How can we go to God for solace, to help us come to terms with whatever bitter loss we are experiencing, if God is in fact the architect of that loss? Can He even help us get through another sleepless night?

Many of us don't lose only the loved one, our health, or our business. Collateral damage includes the loss of our hopes and dreams for the future, plans we made. We might lose our faith in God as well.

If I'm describing you, then this is your book.

Let me tell you my story briefly. I was an Orthodox rabbi, married with eleven children—that's right, eleven! I was the leader of a growing community and the director of a day school, the Hebrew Academy of Huntington Beach in Southern California. When people in my religious community or in our school suffered tragic loss, God forbid, you could say I was the consoler-in-chief.

It was my duty to sit with the families, to listen to them, to see if they wanted an explanation or a hug. I hoped to provide them with the time-honored answers that Judaism has always given to those who were spiraling through tragedy and loss.

I knew all the answers because I was a well-trained rabbi. On many occasions, I was thrust into situations where I had to explain sudden or prolonged loss to community members or members of the school population, such as the tragedy of a twenty-nine-year-old father of three young boys dying from pancreatic cancer. I had to give the answers Judaism provides as to how God could permit such tragedy and suffering to innocent people. I thought those answers were enough to begin the healing process or even to bring about a complete healing.

And then my wife died.

I was thirty-eight and she was thirty-six. We had a wonderful marriage, and as you can see, we took the biblical commandment to *Be fruitful and multiply* very seriously!

Now all eyes were on me. An entire community and an entire school wanted to know: How could God permit something like this? How could a lovely woman like my wife—a person admired and respected in our community and a mother of eleven children, the oldest just fourteen years old—suddenly be taken from us?

People asked, as people ask at those moments: Where is God? How could God permit such a thing? Is there a God? Is God loving? If God is loving, how could this happen?

And for the first time in my life, I had to ask *myself* those questions, but on a deeper level than ever before. When someone else goes through a painful experience, we often say it's a test. But when we ourselves go through such an experience, we tell ourselves it's a tragedy. This is understandable. If we were not emotionally distanced to some degree from the losses of others, we could not get through the day. But when it comes to a loss we suffer personally, there is no such distancing. So now, as I reeled from my wife's sudden passing, I had to ask myself: Did the answers I had been giving others for so long still make sense?

The good news is that they did. Jews have had thousands of years of practice coping with tragedy and loss. Perhaps there is no group of people on earth who have gone through so much for so long! From our enslavement in Egypt to the attempt by the Nazis to annihilate us, not to mention countless expulsions and pogroms in between, we are masters at coping with the worst things that could possibly happen in life. We have been supported through our calamities by timeless Jewish wisdom. We have distilled those bitter experiences into a philosophy and an approach to understand and deal with tragedy. In this book, it is my goal to share those teachings with you.

A while before my wife passed away, a book was published entitled *When Bad Things Happen to Good People* by Rabbi Harold Kushner. The title is a rough approximation of Moses' challenge to God, "Why is there a *tzaddik v'ra lo*?" which literally means "a righteous person to whom bad happens." This challenge is cited in the Talmud.[1]* In one sense, it's a question without an answer, because we can never understand, from our viewpoint as human beings on Planet Earth, exactly what God has in mind. But God has provided plenty of clues that our rabbis were able to decipher and translate into language that humans can understand. Developing these clues is the purpose of this book.

That bestselling book's answer to the timeless issues surrounding *When Bad Things Happen to Good People* is that evil exists because God is not fully in control of the universe. Kushner's view is that there are pockets of untamed evil and chaos that even God has not conquered. This is an intriguing idea, and while the book provided

---

* **Talmud**: A literary work of monumental proportions that draws upon the legal, spiritual, intellectual, ethical, and historical traditions of Judaism. The thirty-seven tractates of the Babylonian Talmud contain the teachings of the Jewish Sages from the period after the destruction of the Second Temple through the fifth century CE. It has served as the primary vehicle for the transmission of the Oral Law and the education of Jews over the centuries; it is the entry point for all subsequent legal, ethical, and theological Jewish scholarship.

comfort to many, to be frank, it is not a Jewish idea. In fact, I'm challenged to even call it a religious idea. We Jews believe that God is firmly in control of every corner of the universe, and, as hard as that may be to understand, bad things *can* happen to decent people.

In a way, it's a simpler course to throw up one's hands and say, "There are forces greater than God, and those forces are to blame for whatever unfortunate or evil thing happens in the world." God's role would then be that of the Sympathizer and Comforter-in-Chief Who sits on the sidelines. But again, that's not a Jewish approach. In this book, we are going to tackle a much more difficult question: How can bad things happen to good people, like the sudden death of my wife, or the loss that you are going through, while we maintain the belief that a loving God is always in charge of the universe?

I won't give you easy answers. There are no easy answers. Instead, I'm going to tap into an almost four-thousand-year-old tradition that has provided comfort, understanding, and ultimately peace to countless individuals throughout the generations.

There may be easier books to read on this subject. There are certainly easier books to write! I started this book over thirty years ago and have struggled with the concepts and the content all this time. As I survey our society today, I'm convinced that, more than ever, people who are suffering after great loss need what we call in Judaism *emes*—the truth, God's Truth. So this a book about the truth: about loss, suffering, and tragedy. It's about God, and ultimately, about hope.

Viktor Frankl,* psychiatrist, founder of the psycho-analytic school of logotherapy, and Holocaust survivor, is often credited with the following quote that affirms his teachings: "Between stimulus and response, there is a space. In that space lies our freedom and our power to choose our response. In our response lies our growth and our happiness." If you're reading this book, it is because you are in the space between the stimulus—the crisis and tragedy you are dealing with—and the response: you feel challenged to integrate and process your painful experience. This is a very personal and sacred space.

I ask that you allow me to join you and share some of my experience and thoughts about this timeless problem. Together we might grow and, ultimately, celebrate the freedom that comes from it. Because this book has been written by someone in tears, someone who suffered such a loss ... for others who have also suffered such a loss.

So take my hand and let us begin.

---

* **Viktor Emil Frankl, 1905–1997:** Founder of logotherapy. Frankl was professor of neurology and psychiatry at the University of Vienna Medical School. During World War II, he spent three years in various concentration camps, including Theresienstadt, Auschwitz, and Dachau. Frankl was the founder of the psychotherapeutic school called logotherapy, and he authored thirty-nine books, which have been published in thirty-eight languages. His most famous book, *Man's Search for Meaning,* has sold over nine million copies in the US alone.

Endnotes:
1   *Brachot* 7a.

CHAPTER ONE

God's Defense Attorney

Little Peter wrote to advice columnist Abigail Van Buren:

DEAR ABBY: My Sunday school teacher says that God is everywhere. Please put this letter in the paper and maybe he will see it.

Dear God: Why did you let my brother die? When he was hit by the car, my mother prayed to you to let him live but you wouldn't. My little brother was only two years old, and he couldn't have sinned so bad that you had to punish him that way. Everyone says you are good and can do anything you want to do. You could have saved my brother, but you let him die. You broke my mother's heart. How can I love you? —Peter[1]

Peter's letter articulates the age-old question: Why do the righteous suffer? Or, in its more updated phrasing: Why do bad things happen to good people?

As adults, we may be more sophisticated and articulate than Peter, but we are not much more advanced than he is in expressing our challenges in dealing with life's apparent injustices.

Peter had been taught that God is all-powerful, and that God is good. He even knows that God listens to our prayers. He is stymied by his little brother's death, which God allowed. He cannot fathom his brother doing something so bad as to warrant such harsh treatment by God. His mother's prayers went unanswered, and he sees her heartbroken. Naturally, he wonders about God: "How can I love You?" As adults, we might wonder, "How can I believe in You?"

When dealing with life's inevitable difficulties and losses, we often react with conclusions such as, "Life is not fair!" or perhaps even, "Life stinks!" This is our way of expressing our anguish and frustration. Others rail in their hearts against what they perceive as God's injustice and may also speak out harshly or cynically against God to their friends who come to support them. These are all ways, among others, by which we protest the unfathomable, seemingly cruel and unjust events in our lives. Either implicitly or explicitly, we blame God and the way He runs the world.

I've had my run-in with God, too.

"Why did God do this to us?"

I was ordained as a rabbi in 1969. I visited the ill—at home, the hospital, and in hospice—always trying to be supportive, to find the appropriate words for each situation. Sometimes it was rather uncomplicated, such as when the person was very old and was gently going into that good night. Other times it was much more difficult. What can you tell a husband whose wife and young daughter were killed by a drunk driver speeding through a pedestrian crosswalk? What do you say to a family whose husband and father just committed suicide? How can you console a young father and mother whose seemingly healthy first child died suddenly from sudden infant death syndrome (SIDS)? What words can offer comfort? What do you answer when they ask, "Why did God do this to us?"

As a young rabbi, I felt that I was meant to be God's defense attorney. Some cases were easier, some harder. My "Client," God, was certainly innocent—of that I was certain—and I had all the answers. It was just a question of finding the right words to fit the situation.

But on that fateful Sunday morning when my young wife—to whom I had been married for sixteen years and who was the mother of our eleven children—died quite suddenly and unexpectedly, things changed. It was the first time in my life that I had encountered death so up close and personally.

Now it was my turn to need comfort and consolation ... and I had more questions than answers. My wife, Rochel Leah, may she rest in peace, was a good person, devoted and devout. Why would God end her life, taking her from her husband and young children on a bright and beautiful sunny Southern California Sunday morning? Was she perfect? Certainly not, but who is? She was as good as many and better than most. She didn't deserve to die at thirty-six.

With overwhelming force, I suddenly realized how

little I truly understood what I had been preaching. In an instant, I gained much more empathy for the loneliness and pain of those whom I had counseled in the past. And about my Client? I wasn't so sure of His absolute innocence anymore. If I were considering cutting a deal, "guilty with an explanation" might be the more appropriate plea.

Convinced they were at fault

Dr. Daniel and Mrs. Shirley Levy lost their young son, Benjamin, to a hot dog. Benny was five years old and eating dinner with his parents when a frankfurter became lodged in his throat and cut off his breathing. His father, a physician, was right there. After trying to dislodge the blockage manually and then through the Heimlich maneuver, he performed an emergency tracheotomy, to no avail. It was too late.

When I visited them, the parents were beaten and very quiet. Although Jewish tradition teaches that when we go to comfort a mourner, we are meant to stay quiet and listen to the mourner speak or wait for them to indicate a desire for us to talk, the Levys didn't speak. They listened as I said what I had said many times before about God's ways being inscrutable, yet those ways certainly having a purpose.

Finally, the bereaved father looked me straight in the eyes and said, "You know, Rabbi, in Manchester, England, where I grew up, I was an observant Jew. I kept kosher—the Jewish dietary laws—and I kept Shabbat. Somewhere over the years, these fell by the wayside..." Dr. Levy trailed off into silence. It took a few moments for me to realize what he was saying: He interpreted his son's loss as a punishment for his having strayed from religious tradition. He was saying that it was his fault! The implication stunned me.

I protested emphatically and assured them both that this tragedy was not God's punishment for Dr. Levy's lapsed observance. Since God's ways are inscrutable, we should not presume to make any such assumptions, or interpret situations like this in a way that encourages self-blame. My rabbinical protestations fell on deaf ears. He was certain about his conclusion—that their son's death was punishment from on high for his religious lapses. I failed to comfort them. Dr. Levy fell into a depression that lasted several months.

But who was right? Did I really know what God's plan was? Doesn't the Talmud say, "He who is beset with affliction should scrutinize his deeds,"[2] and, "There is no affliction without sin?"[3] Doesn't Psalms say, *God is righteous in all his ways*?[4] I certainly couldn't tell them why their bright child was not going to go into the first grade in September. All I could offer was a vague idea about God's transcendent ways. Could they have been right? They had a much more tangible explanation for their loss than I had: that they had offended God, and their son paid the price!

Now, in addition to being bereaved, they were convinced that they were the cause of their son's death. This would explain Daniel's subsequent depression. If depression is a result of unexpressed anger turned inward, then this was a classic example. His British stiff-upper-lip demeanor would not allow him to express anger at God, so it was turned inward.

I had thought and taught that religion is there to support you in your time of need. Well, in this couple's time of need it poured salt on their wounds.

And if this were punishment from God, it would seem entirely misdirected, not to mention disproportionate. Punishment for the father's religious lapse should have been directed toward the father, not his child. Death, we can all agree, seems an unduly harsh response for his infractions.

There is another problem with viewing affliction as a personal punishment. It comes without any indication of why it is happening. Imagine a father becoming aware that his son did something wrong a week earlier, and when he comes home from work that evening, he is very upset and imposes the harshest punishment that is in the family arsenal on his son. However, the only thing he fails to do is tell his son that he is being punished for what he did the week before. The son is left to speculate on why this punishment was coming to him. The son's attention span is limited to the here and now, so he is confused and upset. Whatever benefit might have come from the punishment is entirely lost on him. All it does is engender resentment. Likewise, if one's travail came with an indication of what the person did to deserve the suffering, the individual could certainly get the message and benefit from it. But when suffering seems random, or without any messages attached, we are left bereft and bewildered.

Furthermore, the punishment-for-my-sins premise also seems to be applied entirely capriciously. "Why me?" becomes a very legitimate complaint, because most people who suffer tragedy do not stand out as particularly bad people.

When a tragedy afflicts a truly bad person, we may say, if only under our breaths, *Good riddance, this rotten person got his just deserts.*

But what about us regular people? Most of us are not remarkably bad or remarkably pious. Most of the people I know are basically good. They want to earn an honest living so they can raise their families with sound ethical and moral standards. They work hard to be productive people. Do they make mistakes? Who doesn't? To err is human! Are they perfect? Far from it. But are they basically good? Based on my many decades of knowing people and studying human nature, I would vote yes.

Since we are good but not perfect, we would not have to dig deeply to find things about which we can feel guilty. Some people bask in their imperfections, making a career of sorts out of it. This certainly helps the careers and the bank accounts of their therapists! But surely, we can all be kinder and gentler, especially to those near and dear to us. For example, even after a hard day at work, we should greet our spouses and children with a smile, and not take out the day's frustrations on them through our sour mood. There are many ways we can try to be more "other-focused" and less self-centered, such as committing not to drive faster than the speed limit and to slow down and not speed up when the light turns yellow. We can choose to stop shopping online or checking our personal email while we are working for a client or boss. It's easier than it should be to personalize a list of our habits and traits that could stand some improvement. But is God really such a vengeful, nitpicking deity Who waits to pounce on us when all we are doing is being human?

The question of "Why do bad things happen to good people?" might be more accurately phrased, "Why do tragic and disproportionately bad things happen to ordinary, basically good people?"

I quite understand why the sin=punishment equation is popular. It is simple and neat. God is in charge; He sets the rules. If you break them, you pay. Simple!

Oh, if only it *were* so simple! Far too many corrupt people seem to fly under the radar, getting away with everything from misdemeanors to murder.

God's defenders would say that God is patient but exacts His justice at a later time. This may indeed be true in the Afterlife, but in this world, from what we observe, often it isn't so. How many corrupt people work outside the law and die rich and powerful—and smug? What about the Nazis who escaped to South America or Egypt and died peacefully despite their heinous crimes? Of the more than two hundred thousand perpetrators of Nazi-era crimes, "only six thousand, six hundred fifty-six were convicted."[5] For every Adolph Eichmann who was caught and for whom justice, albeit delayed, ultimately prevailed, the vast majority got away with it—to the very end.

Job, the biblical character most associated with the

suffering of the innocent, agonized about this when he
said:

> *Why do the wicked live, become powerful, and even*
> *amass fortune? ... They said to God, "Go away from*
> *us! We have no desire to know Your ways! What is the*
> *Almighty that we should serve Him? What will we gain*
> *if we pray to Him?"*[6]

Jeremiah, the biblical prophet who consistently
warned the people about the punishments they could
expect by continually flouting God's law, eventually exclaimed in frustration, *Why does the way of the wicked*
prosper, and why are the betrayers tranquil?[7]

It seems that the good, average person bears the brunt
of inexplicable, inequitable suffering.

Feeling abandoned by God

A young woman named Beth became religious as a teenager. She was beautiful and smart. In choosing a religious
path, she also cut herself off from a lot of opportunities
and fun. At nineteen, she went on a summer trip to Israel.
There she fell and came back nursing a broken coccyx. After healing, she continued stumbling and falling and constantly dropping things. She went to her doctor who, after
extensive tests, diagnosed her with multiple sclerosis.

She called me and cried, "I haven't yet lived, and now
this?!" I tried to comfort her and to fortify her with hope.
"Doctors are here to heal, not to condemn," I said to her.
"Prayer is how we petition God to hear us and heal us."

She responded, "First God made me sick and then I

should pray to Him to heal me? What is this, some kind of a cruel and cynical game? If it is, I refuse to play."

Helplessly, I watched her deterioration. First, she used crutches to get around, then a walker. Within two years, Beth was in a wheelchair before finally being confined to bed. Her mother bathed her regularly until one day her mother accidently dropped her, and Beth broke her femur (thigh bone). Overcome by guilt, her mother resigned from being her caretaker and Beth ended up in a nursing home, where her companions were at least fifty years her senior and in poor states not only physically but mentally. Can any of us imagine Beth's level of misery?

When her disease progressed so much that her breathing was compromised and she required a tracheotomy, she refused. Beth wanted to die. Her family asked me to speak to her to convince her to accept the tracheotomy, explaining that since I was the one who helped initiate her spiritual journey, I was the only one she would listen to.

This was one of the hardest moments in my career as a rabbi. When I went to see her, Beth challenged me. "Is this what I get for deciding to be religious? I didn't think about reward for doing the right thing, but why is God making me suffer like this? I gave up so much to be on God's side—why has He abandoned me?"

I had little in my spiritual toolbox at that moment. My sermonette, *My—God's—thoughts are not your thoughts, nor are your ways My ways*,[8] was not well received. She cried, and I cried with her, but I couldn't help her. *Why, indeed?* I asked myself.

That God is beyond man's understanding is obvious and requires no elaboration. But where is He when He is needed most? Where was the kind and merciful God? Why had He been hiding from Beth? Belief in God is so ethereal, and Beth's misery was so tangible. My heart felt very heavy that I couldn't provide an adequate defense for my Client nor offer solace for a formerly vibrant young woman who had chosen me as her spiritual guide.

Another proposed reason for suffering is that God wants to alert people to pay attention to their shortcomings. We get so caught up in living—and living it up—that we can forget what life's purpose is all about. A crisis forces us to pause, reflect, and make adjustments.

Fine, God. You got my attention—by ruining my life!

A friend of mine, a rabbi who serves the community of Palm Beach, Florida, shared with me the travail of many of the elderly in his community. They were living it up the best they could in their seventies until many of them lost it all in the Bernie Madoff Ponzi scheme. They were utterly ruined—financially and emotionally.

My friend quoted one of his acquaintances; let's call him Joseph:

> *Yesterday, I was a* gantze macher *(big shot). After all, I had a few million dollars invested with Madoff, with a nice chunk of change coming in every month. Overnight, I only have enough for the next year or so, and then what? Sure, I realize now that I've been squandering my time on golf and tennis, finding the best new restaurant and other trivial pursuits. Now I realize how little*

> I cared about others, and that I was not very charita-
> ble. My synagogue attendance did not increase after I
> retired, despite what I had promised myself during my
> heyday, and I still attend only on the High Holidays
> and an occasional bar mitzvah. Fine, God! You got my
> attention, and you did it by ruining the rest of my life!

Shaking someone to wake them from their sleep is important if they are sleeping their years away, but to shake
them so violently that they break their necks is criminal.
I would say to God that, if disasters happen because You
want to redirect a person, make sure that when You're
finished, the individual is still intact and is not a broken,
ruined person.

To refine and ennoble

Many believers in God explain that the purpose of human
suffering is to refine us, to ennoble us, to make us more
sensitive to those less fortunate. Simplistic as this may be,
every time I get a bad cold, which is infrequent, I remind
myself, "When you are in good health, you become insensitive to those who are in pain, and so many people are in
constant, sometimes excruciating, pain." This sensitivity,
at least for me, lasts for a few weeks before it recedes to
my subconscious.

And then I think of my friend Eleanor, who joyously
married her college sweetheart, a promising law student.
At the end of their first year of marriage, while they waited for the results of his bar exam, they chose to gallivant
through Europe by car. Their first weeks were excellent—
until their rented car skidded off a mountain road in It-

aly and hit a tree. Her husband suffered minor injuries, but Eleanor's injuries were very severe. After a long delay for medical personnel to reach the remote area, the police had to complete a criminal investigation before they would allow them to fly to a hospital in Milan that had the facilities to treat her injures. By the time she got there, the damage was permanent. Eleanor had become a paraplegic.

I have known this woman for more than thirty years, and I can tell you that her pain and misery didn't ennoble her; they embittered her. She became dependent on her husband and others, lost her dignity and sense of self-worth, and eventually lost her marriage, too. Where was the refinement and reawakening that was supposed to be the result of the suffering? This scenario and others, tragically similar, have been repeated endlessly throughout time. You can probably think of at least one "Eleanor" in your own life.

Afflictions of love

Another source of human suffering is called afflictions of love,[9] in which God refines the truly righteous, so that when they die and their souls go to heaven, they will have been especially "scoured" to become pristine and thoroughly prepared to be ushered into heaven. This is supported by the verse, *For God admonished the one He loves, and like a father He mollifies the child.*[10] Since this "reason" for human suffering is rare and unique, I'm not going to elaborate. I will just add that reading this book, particularly chapter 9, will provide context for this concept.

Is suffering a test we can pass?

Have you heard about the "test theory" concerning suffering? It goes like this: God wants to test our mettle and find out who we truly are. Suffering is a test that challenges us to rise to the occasion.

This idea can be found in the Bible: *For God, your Lord, tests you in order to know whether you love God, your Lord, with all your heart and with all your* soul... .[11] *... in order to afflict you and to test you to do good for you in the end.*[12]

This is what happened to long-suffering Job (more about him later). He was certifiably a good person; God attested to it. Then the Satan* cynically said to God, "He's good because he's got it made. Give him to me to do with him as I please, and then You'll see how truly faithful he'll be when he loses it all."[13]

The problem here is that many of those who pass the test and remain faithful and pious throughout do not experience the *to do good for you in the end*. Then there are the many who find the test too difficult and say, I didn't sign up for this, and drop out. Actually, they stomp out, angry and bitter at God.

---

* In Jewish theology, the Satan, often translated as the Adversary, is a holy, Godly angel whose task in his service of God is to be the contrarian. He challenged God about Job's righteousness and had God agree to hand Job over to his adversarial dominion. He is also the source of what Judaism calls the evil inclination, the force within us that entices us away from the path of goodness. He is also the Angel of Death, whose mission is to take a person's soul when his or her lifespan on earth is up. That is what the Talmud means in saying, "Satan the adversary, the evil inclination, and the Angel of Death are one; that is, they are three aspects of the same essence." (*Bava Batra* 16a).

The Jewish answer is that it is all balanced out in the Afterlife. The totality of our existence is not limited to the seventy, eighty, ninety, or more years we spend in this earthly existence. When a person dies, the body is ensconced in the earth, but the soul goes to heaven and is judged. Even good people must be cleansed from the grime that attached to them while here. And even the wicked must be rewarded for whatever good they've done.

The good people who suffer in this world will receive their just rewards in heaven, after their necessary "cleansing." But the wicked who have enjoyed a good time here go straight to hell when they die, because they've already taken their reward in their earthly lives.

What's wrong with this answer? It's certainly logical. One problem is that the suffering in this life is very real and very painful. The promise of a final future reckoning is too abstract to serve as an adequate answer. Just as a hungry person cannot be fed with a rich idea, it is difficult for an abstract concept to serve as balm for real pain.

Even if I were able to come to terms with God's decisions regarding individuals, such as Peter's little brother, or Joseph, Beth, and Eleanor, or five-year-old Benjamin, how can I explain to myself and others God's plan when disaster befalls an entire group of people?

What can we say when we hear of a tourist bus that drove off a cliff, killing all sixty aboard, because the driver fell asleep or because the brakes failed? Did God have something against the driver and each one of the fifty-nine passengers?

Canary Islands air disaster

On March 27, 1977, two Boeing 747 airliners, Pan Am Flight 1736 with three hundred ninety-six aboard, and KLM Flight 4805 with two hundred forty-eight aboard (including forty-eight children and three infants), collided on the runway of Los Rodeos Airport on the Spanish island of Tenerife, resulting in the deaths of five hundred eighty-three people. It became the worst accident in aviation history. On the Pan Am flight, three hundred sixty-six passengers had boarded in Los Angeles, and fourteen had boarded in New York. All of the two hundred thirty-four passengers on the KLM flight boarded in the Netherlands. Most were Dutch, but four Germans, two Australians, and two US citizens were also on board. The original destination of both planes was Las Palmas de Gran Canaria Airport on the neighboring island of Gran Canaria, but the flights were diverted to Tenerife because a terrorist bomb had exploded in the terminal of the airport in Las Palmas. Of the six hundred twenty-eight passengers, the vast majority of whom were presumably going on vacation to the Canary Islands, only fifty-two survived.

Are we to understand that God assembled all these people from different cities and countries because they were destined to die in the inferno resulting from the head-on collision of the two planes? Are we to make of this that God's Angel of Death does wholesale? This just boggles the mind.

And what are we to think of the fifty-two passengers and nine crew members of the Pan Am flight who survived? Were they just lucky? Or was it simply that their time was not up yet? And what should we make of Robina van Lanschot, who arrived with KLM Flight 4805 in Tenerife but elected not to reboard it, and was the sole surviving passenger of that plane? Robina was a tour guide who lived in Puerto de la Cruz on Tenerife Island and wanted to see her boyfriend that night. Was her decision to spend the night with her boyfriend Divinely inspired? Or should we just say that it was her good luck?

What about the two thousand, six hundred thirty people who perished in the terrorist attacks on the Twin Towers at the World Trade Center on the infamous day of September 11, 2001? What can we make of the many people who were scheduled to work in those towers that day but for whatever reason didn't come to work and were spared? Were they lucky, too, or were they simply marked for survival? Far greater casualties resulted from the massive Asian tsunami of December 26, 2004, killing a staggering two hundred twenty-five thousand people in eleven countries. The larger the casualty numbers, the more we are stunned, pained, and likely to ask: What was God thinking?

Letting God off the hook

Earlier, we mentioned the philosophy that was set out in the book, *When Bad Things Happen to Good People,* which is that God is not responsible for everything that happens to us. Kushner's philosophy is that though He created the world and set in place certain moral principles for human beings to follow, He simply doesn't have a complete level of control over events that happen in His world. When bad things happen to good people, He takes on the role of Sympathizer-in-Chief. That's the best He can do. Therefore, God is not the source of the suffering and is powerless to stop it. Kushner lets God off the hook.

A more extreme version of this philosophy is that of Deism, the belief in the existence of a supreme being, but one that does not intervene in the universe. This philosophy emerged in the seventeenth and eighteenth centuries, based on the "reasonable" assumption that the world required a creator, but they rejected the belief that the creator interacts with its creations.

Kushner's perspective is novel. Generally, the challenge of suffering lies in the difficulty of reconciling three postulates:

1. God is all-powerful, or omnipotent.
2. God is all-good, or omnibenevolent.
3. There is unwarranted suffering.

The problem becomes clear. If God is all-powerful and all-good, there should not be unwarranted suffering. God should not allow it to happen. We have a few choices in how to reconcile the three:

1. Either the suffering *is* warranted and justified and therefore compatible with an all-powerful and all-good God.
2. God *is* all-powerful and the suffering *is* bad, but God is *not* good.
3. The suffering is real and bad, God *is* good, but God is not all-powerful. He's not even powerful enough to stop the evil in His world; hence, people suffer.

The usual efforts to answer the question of why the good suffer hold God's omnipotence and omnibenevolence as sacrosanct. After all, what kind of God would He be if He were not powerful and good? This leaves the only answer: that the suffering is *somehow* not bad. The attitude that God cannot stop the forces that cause the suffering—Kushner's postulate— may seem novel and refreshing. It also breaks new ground for the ones suffering. "It's not God's fault," they say, "He can't help it either." Rather, God is alongside the victims and empathizes with them, but there's nothing He can do about it.

The problem with the idea of God having limited powers is that if He cannot stop the evil that causes innocents to suffer, how and why can He be responsible for the good that happens to us? If He is the Creator, does He not dominate His own creation? If He is not predominant in all matters, surely we'd have to excise the phrase "Thank God" from our lexicon, since God would therefore not be responsible for the good either. What thanks would we owe Him? Even as he was writhing in the pain of his suffering, Job said to his wife, *Shall we accept the good from God and not accept the bad?*[14]

To give God credit for the good in our lives, but not to consider Him responsible for the bad, is a bit like religious gerrymandering—a political ploy of manipulating the boundaries of an electoral constituency to benefit one party based on considerations other than geography. Self-serving gerrymandering can warp a political system, and it can warp and confuse theological boundaries as well. It doesn't work in either system.

One might say that those who negate God's power because that's the only way they can come to terms with suffering render their God to be impotent.

In this chapter, I have introduced several approaches for why bad things happen to good people. These reasons attempt to reconcile how God can allow such things to happen while still remaining a God Who is all-powerful and still good. These explanations are known as theodicies,* and understanding them will offer a useful framework for the rest of the book's ideas.

The theodicies I've introduced in this chapter, and which will be developed further in this book, are that the goals of suffering, despite being in God's created world, are: a) for refinement of one's character; b) as punishment for personal sins; c) as afflictions of love; d) as a test of faith; and e) suffering that remains beyond a mortal's understanding but will be ameliorated in the Afterlife. One more—f) suffering related to a previous incarnation—will be discussed in later chapters.

These are profound and sometimes profoundly challenging ideas. While all the aforementioned theodicies are sourced and deemed true in Jewish philosophy, their application to any specific tragic event is elusive by design. In other words, all of these reasons are legitimate,

---

* *Theodicy* is from the Greek *theos*, meaning god, and *dikē* meaning justice, trial, or judgment. Theodicy literally means justifying God, and it is an explanation of why a perfectly good, almighty, and all-knowing God permits evil.

but we cannot know which of them, or which combination of them, might be *the* reason behind *our* individual suffering. We also cannot determine the proportionality of any of them. How any combination of these theodicies might play out in a given instance of human suffering is something only God can know.

Chapter Summary: *There are many philosophical models about why God can be perfectly good, almighty, and all-knowing and yet still allow suffering. While some argue that perhaps God isn't really that good or that powerful, Judaism believes that suffering has an ultimate purpose. In fact, it is actually good, but in a way that is beyond our comprehension because our human understanding is so limited. Working toward an understanding of God's role in suffering can be an engine for personal and spiritual growth.*

Endnotes:

1   "Dear Abby" by Abigail Van Buren, a syndicated advice columnist.
2   *Brachot* 5a.
3   *Shabbat* 55a.
4   Psalms 145:17.
5   *Reckonings: Legacies of Nazi Persecution and the Quest for Justice* by
     Professor Mary Fulbrook (New York: Oxford University Press, 2018), as
     reviewed in "Historian Exposes Germany's Minute Number of Convic-
     tions for Nazi War Crimes," Times of Israel, November 10, 2018.
6   Job 21:7, 14–15.
7   Jeremiah 12:1.
8   Isaiah 55:8.
9   *Brachot* 5a.
10   Proverbs 2:12.
11   Deuteronomy 13:4.
12   Ibid. 8:16.
13   Job 1:9–11 (paraphrased).
14   Job 2:10.

CHAPTER TWO

The Challenge of Living with Evil

A young man came to his rabbi and told him, "I don't believe in God anymore."

The rabbi was unperturbed. "Tell me about the God you don't believe in," the rabbi said calmly, "because I might not believe in that God either."

Before attempting to address the challenges raised in the last chapter, I need to ask you a question. In trying to come to terms with a tragedy, what kind of answer would satisfy you? Would a perfectly rational answer—assuming one can be found—give you peace? In a Philosophy 101 class, perhaps, but in real life? I doubt it.

The reason that no satisfactory answer exists to the question, "Where was God when this terrible thing happened?" is simple. The questions each of us have in the face of a tragedy do not come from the mind—the intellectual part of ourselves. The questions come from the heart—the seat of our emotions—or from the gut. Intellectual answers, profound though they may be, do not speak the language of the heart. What *does* speak to the heart? Perhaps language may not be sufficient at all.

Back in the 1980s, my friend and colleague Rabbi Shlomo Schwartz told me about a lecture he had attended given by Elie Wiesel, the renowned Holocaust survivor,

writer, lecturer, professor, and Nobel Peace Prize winner.∗ Rabbi Schwartz was the Chabad representative at
the UCLA campus, and what he told me about Wiesel's
remarks resonated so strongly that I have never forgotten it. A young audience member continued to taunt the
speaker with the question, "And where was God?" Finally,
tired of the interruptions, Wiesel replied, "And if I answer
you, will that make things good?"

Do you want an answer, or do you want a hug?

I was once visiting one of my sons, a rabbi in Atlanta. We
went out one evening to talk. He vented to me about what
was happening to his cousin—my nephew, also a rabbi—
who had been diagnosed with lung cancer and was apparently losing the battle. My son spoke to me about how
good a human being my nephew was, that he had a young
and growing family, and how difficult and unfair the situation was for everyone. I listened patiently as he poured
his heart out.

As he was speaking, I began formulating my rabbinic
response; after all, I had done this countless times before.
Then I realized that he is a rabbi, too. He's been confronted with these very same issues and has the wisdom of life
and the wisdom of the sages to offer, just as I do. What

∗ **Elie Wiesel, 1928–2016**: Writer and activist. Wiesel was born in
Sighet, Romania, and was deported by the Nazis to Auschwitz when he was
fifteen. He wrote more than forty books of fiction and nonfiction, including
the acclaimed memoir *Night*, which has been published in more than thirty languages. In 1986, Wiesel won the Nobel Prize for Peace. He received
numerous awards, including the Presidential Medal of Freedom and the US
Congressional Gold Medal.

purpose is there in telling him that which he already knows?

When I had an opportunity to respond, I looked into his eyes and said, "Eliyahu, do you want an answer, or do you want a hug?" I caught him off guard, and he took a few moments to respond. His eyes filled with tears, and finally he said, "I want a hug."

A person in pain is a person who really wants the pain to go away. Sometimes a hug serves that need much better than any verbal answer could. Most grown men don't know how to ask for a hug, so they camouflage their needs under the guise of wanting an answer. But there's a time to philosophize and a time to embrace, and the trick is knowing which one you need at any given time. The wrong response, whether it's from the head or the heart, can often make things worse.

Before the answer, before the hug, there is just the human being, the tragedy, and God. If you were faced with tragedy, you might address God with anger and reproach. You might raise your hands and yell at the heavens, demanding to know how God could allow this tragedy to happen. You might rant and rave at the God you once called merciful to explain how such evil could come into your life. You are protesting the events and, implicitly or explicitly, blaming God and the way He runs the world.

This type of response is understandable, but when people engage in ranting and angry rhetoric, they actually do themselves a great disservice. How so? By framing their circumstances in a depressed and bitter light, it becomes harder for them to extricate themselves from their predicament. Instead, that person should heed what some call "The First Law of Holes": *When you find yourself in a hole, quit digging.*

After suffering losses of biblical proportions, Job's wife says to him in exasperation, *Job, blaspheme—and die!* Job's response? *You talk as an impious woman might talk; furthermore, shall we accept the good from God and not accept the bad?* The Scripture goes on to say: *Despite everything, Job did not sin with his lips.*[1] This means that even under his most horrendous circumstances, Job did not criticize God, nor would he accept his wife's angry language.

The Talmud does not exactly justify displays of bitterness toward God, but it is sympathetic to human frailties and accommodates them. It states compassionately, "A person is not culpable for blasphemy expressed when grieving."[2]

In fact, Judaism has a rich tradition of leaders who challenged God's ways. When God tells Abraham, the first Jew, that He intends to destroy the wicked city of Sodom for the cruelty and immorality of its inhabitants, Abraham counters, *It would be sacrilege to You [to bring death to the righteous along with the guilty].*[3] When Pharaoh punishes the Israelites after Moses' first challenging encounter with the Egyptian ruler, Moses rebukes God, saying, *Why do You mistreat this people?*[4] And again, when God threatens to destroy the Israelites after they had forged the idolatrous golden calf, Moses pleads, *Forgive them! And if not, please erase me from Your book [the*

Torah] that You have written![5] A yearning for justice and fairness is in the Jewish DNA. Jews throughout history have been drawn toward missions intended to right previous wrongs and to further justice for the underdog and the oppressed.

Then there is the folk tale of Rabbi Levi Yitzchak of Berditchev,* who "summoned" God to a *din Torah,* a lawsuit, wherein he represented the Jews as plaintiffs, challenging the idea that God is acting in a kind and just manner. Rabbi Levi Yitzchak's "lawsuit" against God accused the Almighty of not fulfilling the dictates as set out in the Torah to alleviate the suffering of widows, orphans, the poor, and the downtrodden. His challenge to God was immortalized in a folk song:

> *Good morning to You, Lord, Master of the universe.*
>
> *I, Levi Yitzchak son of Sarah of Berditchev ...*
>
> *I come to You with a* din Torah *from Your people Israel.*
>
> *What do You want of Your people Israel?*
>
> *What have You demanded of Your people Israel?*
>
> *For everywhere I look it says, "Say to the Children of Israel."*
>
> *And every other verse says, "Speak to the Children of Israel."*
>
> *And over and over, "Command the Children of Israel."*

---

* **Rabbi Levi Yitzchak of Berditchev**, 1740–1809: Chasidic rebbe. Rabbi Levi Yitzchak was one of the foremost disciples of the Maggid of Mezritch and later went on to serve as rabbi in Berditchev, Ukraine. His Chasidic commentary on the Torah, *Kedushat Levi*, is a classic that is popular to this day. He is known in Jewish history and folklore for his all-encompassing love, compassion, and advocacy on behalf of the Jewish people.

Father, sweet Father in heaven,

How many nations are there in the world?

Persians, Babylonians, Edomites ...

The Russians, what do they say?

That their czar is the only ruler.

The Prussians, what do they say?

That their Kaiser is supreme.

And the English, what do they say?

That their king is sovereign.

And I, Levi Yitzchak son of Sarah of Berditchev, say,

"Yisgadal v'yiskadash shmei rabbah—

Exalted and hallowed be His great Name."

And I, Levi Yitzchak son of Sarah of Berditchev, say,

"From my stand I will not waver,

And from my place I shall not move

Until there is an end to all this.

Yisgadal v'yiskadash shemei rabbah—

Exalted and hallowed be His great Name."

"God, we're in the world together, forever."

At first blush, Rabbi Levi Yitzchak's summoning God to a *din Torah* might sound arrogant and blasphemous. Could someone of his religious stature actually reject or disavow God, or reduce God to the level of a human being whom one could take to court? But he was not doing any of those things. Instead, his action was an act of love and fidelity, conveying the intimacy of the relationship between the Creator and His chosen people. He was saying, "God, we're in the world together, forever. I have a problem with the way You are dealing with things. Because you know that I subscribe to the same values that You subscribe to, I demand that You live up to the standards that You have set out. Therefore, I can summon You to a *din Torah*."

Rabbi Levi Yitzchak understood that he had standing to challenge God because of the precedents he knew so well from the Torah, and because of the unbreakable bond between God and the Jewish people. This tradition of challenging God, which we first see with the patriarch Abraham, tells us that we should not hesitate to turn to God in our moments of need or when we question what appears to us to be an injustice. Despite the danger of our getting temporarily carried away by our own angry rebuke or negative rhetoric, these heartfelt outcries underscore our belief in God. Even our impassioned ravings attest to the depth of our love for the Almighty. A human being only cries out passionately to someone with whom that person is truly and intimately engaged. Turning to God, even with a critical and angry tone, brings God into the conversation and opens the door for meaningful dialogue with the Creator.

As Elie Wiesel eloquently said, "The Jew ... may rise against God, provided that he remains within God. For a Jew to believe in God is good. For a Jew to protest against God is still good. But to simply ignore God, that is not good. Anger, yes. Protest, yes. Affirmation, yes. But indifference to God, no. You can be a Jew with God; you can be a Jew against God; but not without God."[6]

Anger is something we express in the early stages of traumatic loss or after witnessing wholesale loss of life, whether through illness, an accident, or a massive natural disaster, such as the Asian tsunami. Anger is immediate and raw. A tidal wave of emotion builds and bursts as we lash out against God. Anger is blind, exhausting, and all-encompassing, leaving little room for contemplation or discussion. It is visceral and primal. This anger permeates every cell of our being as it rails and cries out to a God we can only hope is listening.

But after the anger, after the dust of the emotional storm settles, we are left with the most difficult part: to contemplate the *why* of it all. We are all yelled out, and now we are questioning: *Why, God? Why did you allow this tragedy to come into my life? Why should I suffer so? What did I do to deserve this?* Why did hundreds of innocents have to die in that horrible plane crash? Why did Nava Applebaum, a twenty-year-old bride-to-be, and her father, renowned emergency department physician David Applebaum, have to be murdered in a terrorist attack in Jerusalem the night before her wedding?

What is evil? Does it really exist?

Once we ask the questions, we want answers.

You may sit and take in the rabbi's sympathetic words, accept the silence that lets you know he is there for you, and accept his hug. But we still demand some answers.

But before we are prepared to hear answers, we must

first understand what we are really asking. To frame our questions, we must take a step back and look at what we call "bad" or "evil." What is evil, and does it really exist? If it does exist, does the existence of evil conflict with God's goodness or compromise God's power?

The problem with evil, when we contemplate it through a theological lens, can be boiled down to simple logic. As we've discussed, Judaism believes:

1. God is all-powerful. He has not withdrawn from us, and He runs the world as He pleases.
2. God is good. He manages the world with goodness and justice.
3. Evil exists and is real. We know it historically, and we experience it today.

It seems logical that you can have any two of the three, but not all three. If God is all-powerful and runs the world with goodness and justice, *there can be no evil.* If God is all-powerful, and yet evil is real, *then God cannot be good.* If God is good and evil is real, *then God cannot be all-powerful.*

But what if the premise is flawed? Does the presence of an omnipotent, benevolent God actually preclude the existence of evil?

To answer this question, we need to look at Scripture, where God says, *I form light and create darkness; I make peace and create evil. I, God, do all these things.*[7] When reading this verse, many philosophers ask: Is darkness really a creation, or is it the absence of light? And is evil really a creation of God, or is it the absence of good? The prophet seems to say that both darkness and evil are *cre-*

ations; they are not the absence of their opposites. God Himself created them.

If we look deeper, we can begin to understand that darkness and evil are creations that *had* to be made. Why were they necessary? We need darkness to show us the importance of light, and we need evil to show us the value of good. Evil in and of itself has no constructive purpose. However, evil has purpose when it is used as a foil for good, to make goodness meaningful, purposeful, and worthwhile. As they say in Hawaii: no rain, no rainbows!

But evil serves another purpose, as well. In addition to teaching us to value what is good, evil shapes a necessary aspect of an important feature of who we are as human beings: our free choice. The most significant form of evil is the evil that lurks in the heart of human beings. Without this evil, all people would be nice and sweet, following their inborn instinct to do good. But what would the purpose of creation be if we were born perfectly good?

God tells us both before and after the Flood that the nature of human beings is evil from their youth.[8] Evil is, in fact, the human being's default position. Pardon the bluntness, but Job[9] says: *Man is born as a wild ass!* Babies and small children are by nature self-centered and uncivilized until they gain maturity and self-discipline. The three-year-old who is denied a treat and yells, "Mommy, I hate you!" is expressing her undeveloped human nature which every caring parent works to develop and transform their child into, a responsible, moral person. Not everyone is fortunate to have such parents.

Human nature tends toward selfishness and self-aggrandizement, which are not in themselves evil. In tech talk, they are a feature, not a bug—they were deliberately designed and built into us so that we can have the challenge—and ultimately the achievement—of overcoming them. However, people who give themselves license to pursue their selfishness and self-aggrandizement often cross the line into evil. They become evil in the social sense of not caring whom they offend and hurt, and in the moral sense of crossing the line of where their rights end and the rights of others begin.

We are in this world to win the battle over ourselves.

Consider the saying, sometimes attributed to Supreme Court Justice Oliver Wendell Holmes: "My right to swing my hands ends at the tip of your nose." The person who remains evil doesn't care where your nose is and won't stop swinging. Once people have gotten away with doing something evil once or twice, they will be encouraged by the lack of consequences to descend further down the path of hurting others and to take what doesn't belong to them. The Talmud supports this understanding of human nature: "Rav Huna says, 'When a person transgresses and repeats his transgression, it is permitted to him.'" The Talmud challenges this statement: "Can it enter your mind that the transgression is permitted to him because he has sinned twice?" It answers its own question by saying, "It means that it becomes *as if* it were permitted to him," because he becomes accustomed to this behavior and no longer senses that it is a sin.[10]

Now, if we understand that this is the instinctual nature of man, we are one step closer to understanding that an important element of our purpose is to fight our evil instincts and to strive to be good, understanding, and self-less. The purpose of our existence in this world is *to win the battle over ourselves.*

And this is why, the Torah tells us, God allows evil to exist: *so that human beings can choose between good and evil behavior.* If we didn't have to fight the battle for good, we would never own the goodness of our character. Being good would be automatic and therefore meaningless. By creating evil, God gave us something to strive for—to do good by our own volition and initiative.

Animals are not expected to act outside of their in-stincts. We have all seen videos of wild animals killing each other, and nobody considers that bad behavior. By instinct, animals hunt, kill, and eat other animals. We accept that predators will be predators without judging them.

Humans are predatory animals too, in some ways, but humans were charged with a unique responsibility. They were created by God, in the image of God.[11] What does that phrase mean—"in the image of God"? We are not ethereal; we are physical. We are not omnipotent; we have limited powers and authority. The "image" we are talking about isn't about any physical resemblance, which does not exist. But while we are not omnipotent as God is, we have been created with the power to choose. This power, this autonomy, this agency, is Godly. Who has freedom of choice other than human beings?

Rabbi Moshe ben Maimon,* also known as Maimonides, one of the greatest of Torah expositors, who lived in the twelfth century, spelled this out in his *Guide for the Perplexed.*[12] He says that "God created man in His image," means that God gave man the kind of intelligence that allows for freedom of choice. Until God's creation of humanity, only God Himself had this freedom of choice. And what was God's purpose in sharing this gift? It was so that humankind could harness, channel, and conquer its nature for the service of God.

That doesn't mean people should become hermits and live in caves in order to avoid making mistakes. It means that people should live in the world and demonstrate to themselves and to those around them that they can choose to rise above their natures.

This is the human mission. This is why evil exists: so that every individual has the potential to choose morality, generosity, kindness, and even greatness. All people have the potential to strive to override the innate selfishness of their first years of life.

My father, may he rest in peace, had tenants who lived

---

* **Rabbi Moshe ben Maimon (Maimonides, Rambam) 1135–1204:** Halachist, philosopher, author, and physician. Maimonides was born in Córdoba, Spain. After the conquest of Córdoba by the Almohads, he fled Spain and eventually settled in Cairo, Egypt. There, he became the leader of the Jewish community and served as court physician to the vizier of Egypt. He is most noted for authoring the *Mishneh Torah*, an encyclopedic arrangement of Jewish law, and for his philosophical work, *Guide for the Perplexed*. His rulings on Jewish law are integral to the formation of halachic consensus.

downstairs from us. One Thursday night, the woman of the home was cooking and preparing for Shabbat, and suddenly the kitchen faucet popped off its base, sending a geyser of water from the sink to the ceiling, flooding the entire kitchen. Her husband wasn't a very handy person, and he didn't know what to do. Panicking, he ran upstairs and cried out, "Mr. Schusterman, Mr. Schusterman, help, help! The water! It's all over!" My father, seeing the urgency, immediately went downstairs. My father, who was handy, knew that the first thing to do was to turn off the valve under the sink to stop the water from spouting out.

With the water off, the tenant's kitchen was no longer getting soaked. At this point, at 10:30 on a Thursday night, my father could have gone back upstairs and left the sink as it was until he could call a plumber the next day. But he didn't do that. He said, "Don't worry, I'll take care of it." He came back twenty minutes later with his toolbox, his wrenches, and a replacement faucet. He took off the tenant's old faucet, installed the new one, and tested it. The new faucet worked, and by 11:30 that night, the tenants had their water running smoothly again.

The next day, Friday afternoon, the same tenant came upstairs with a question on an unrelated matter, while my parents were both sitting in their kitchen. The tenant casually looked at my parents' sink and noticed that there was duct tape wrapped around the base of the faucet. Looking a little closer, he exclaimed, "Mr. Schusterman, why did you take off your faucet and put it on my sink and put my broken faucet on your sink?"

My father didn't know how to respond. But my mother, who was sitting there watching the drama, said, "You know, we grew up in Russia where nothing worked, so it is okay if our sink doesn't work so well. You are an American; you are used to having everything work, so now your sink is working. Don't worry, my husband will get us another faucet next week."

My father nodded and said nothing as the tenant stared in amazement.

My father conquered the instinctual self-centered nature that would lead most people to do the minimum required of them. He went further, applying his freedom of choice in the service of goodness, of selflessness. While his act may have been relatively small, its impact was outsized. He took the self-centeredness God had created in this world and conquered it with an act of goodness. Evil may be our default setting, but we can use our precious God-given freedom of choice to fight that tendency and strive to do good.

Yes, evil *does* exist, and it is not just the absence of good. Instead, *evil is its own entity*, one that was put into this world in order to give us the opportunity to fight it. Human beings must do battle against it every day. It may be the most mixed blessing possible in life, because what may be seen as a curse is actually our blessing. Our opportunity—our challenge to override evil—contributes to our life's purpose. *Without evil, we would not have had the ability to exercise our free choice to choose goodness.*

But what happens when evil isn't a human characteristic to fight but a force that attacks? What happens when the evil comes and punches you in the gut as pain, suffering, or tragedy? How can we overcome an evil that is external to us, active and vicious: one that seems to get its own way no matter what we do? This is what we will explore in the next chapter.

Chapter Summary: *Evil was created by God to ultimately foster good. Despite the devastation it causes, the forces of evil create our motivation to be good and to make moral choices. We can only appreciate the meaning of "light" when we have known "dark," and we can only appreciate goodness when we have known its opposite. We are born selfish, with our own evil instincts. As we grow spiritually, we are challenged to rise above those instincts, practicing the choice of doing good until it becomes our second nature.*

Endnotes:

1   Job 2:10.
2   *Bava Batra* 16b.
3   Genesis 18:25.
4   Exodus 5:22.
5   Exodus 32:32.
6   *First Person Singular,* an interview with Elie Wiesel (PBS Home Video, 2002), DVD.
7   Isaiah 45:7.
8   Genesis 6:5; 8:21.
9   Job 11:12.
10   *Kiddushin* 40a.
11   Genesis 1:27.
12   Maimonides, *Guide for the Perplexed*, Section 1, Chapter 1.

CHAPTER THREE

What Is Evil,
And Why Does It Exist?

I am the One Who forms light and creates dark-
ness; Who makes peace and creates evil; I am God,
Maker of all these.

—Isaiah 45:7

In Chapter 1, we questioned how God can allow evil to exist in the world if He is not only omnipotent, but also omnibenevolent. How can a God who is all-good permit a world where people get sick and sometimes debilitated, or die and leave families and loved ones behind, bereaved and grieving? How can God allow people to suffer injury, death, and incalculable damage from natural disasters? How does He allow evil people to commit violent and destructive acts against their fellow human beings?

Our response, which we introduced in Chapter 2, is that God allows evil in our world—in fact, God *created* evil—in order to challenge human beings to become better and thereby make the world better. If evil didn't exist, and therefore bad things would never happen in the world, we would be good naturally from birth and throughout our lives. However, our goodness would be automatic, passive, unchallenged, and unearned. We would have no choice but to be good.

The existence of evil may be a general and abstract idea, but the evil things that happen to us are personal and specific. The noblest response to evil is to fight against it. This is where heroes are made.

The painful irony of life is that if we did not experience evil, we wouldn't be able to recognize the need for good and would never learn how to be virtuous. We would have no heroes, because heroism would not be necessary.

Can you imagine such a world? It would be peaceful, but we would all feel purposeless. We might all just die of boredom!

As we gain more maturity and life experience, we realize that our own actions often contain a blend of both good and bad, or perhaps in some cases, even a bit of evil. Life is complex. Our motivations are seldom entirely all one thing or the other. We are all a work in progress.

The presence of evil is also what allows human beings to experience free choice. It teaches us to prioritize our good conscience over our bad instincts. For example, most of us conclude, "It's more important for me to contribute to the welfare of our nation by paying taxes than to just enrich myself." Contributing to the public good focuses us on the need to help maintain society, which includes millions of people we don't know and will never know. We understand that no society can survive if each of us maintains a Darwinian survival-of-the-fittest mentality, where our only concern is for ourselves.

Unlike all other living creatures that operate on instinct, God grants human beings consciousness about our actions. This consciousness gives us the ability to overrule instinct and choose between selfishness and selflessness, and between good and evil. With practice, we can develop the habit of choosing goodness, and then goodness becomes part of us. This is how we grow morally, spiritually, and emotionally.

This—the freedom and ability to override our instincts and desires through consciously choosing good—is what is meant when we say that God created man in His own image. God wants us to emulate Him.[1] The Talmud explains: "Just as He is called 'Gracious,' you shall be gracious; just as He is called 'Merciful,' you shall be merciful; just as He is called 'Holy,' you shall be holy."[2] In this chapter, we will unpack the concept that as we develop more self-understanding and God-consciousness, we dedicate ourselves to a higher purpose. We partner with God in making His world a better place.

Will you let your background crush you, or will it spur you on to greatness?

We struggle to understand why God allows us to suffer. When we suffer, we become myopic, unable to see beyond our own experience and grief. After a traumatic event that generates emotional or physical pain, we might see it as a random, isolated incident. But a Jew is meant to view even these incredibly painful circumstances in a broader context. At that moment of crisis, it can be too formidable a challenge to be able to remember one's role as an integral individual on the world's stage. We can't even think in terms of our relationship with God and His teachings, let alone God's larger plan for humankind.

Many events are experienced as tragic or even life-shattering, but as time passes and the situation evolves, the event that was initially so devastating can be seen in a different light. At times it may be revealed, at least in part, as a blessing in disguise.*

I have a colleague who caught a bad cold, which then developed into bronchitis. He coughed constantly and so hard that he broke a rib, which made the pain of coughing even worse. But breaking a rib meant he had to stop smoking cigarettes while his chest was taped up. During those two weeks he was forced to curtail his two-pack-a-day smoking habit, and after going through the worst of the nicotine addiction withdrawal, he decided to stop smoking permanently—probably the best thing that he could have done for his health.

I will now make a statement that some readers will find unnerving, upsetting, or maybe even crazy, but here it is: Based on everything I have experienced in life, including the traumatic loss of my own dear wife at a young age, and based on all that I have studied and learned to be true, I believe that there is no such thing as an *absolutely* bad occurrence. How bad something is will depend on our perspective, and that perspective is likely to be limited.

This point is underscored by the following quote from the Previous Lubavitcher Rebbe, Rabbi Yosef Yitzchak Schneersohn.** After battling the communist regime by

---

* See, for example, the stories in Harvey Mackay's book, *We Got Fired! ... And It's the Best Thing That Ever Happened to Us* (New York: Ballantine Books, 2004).

** **Rabbi Yosef Yitzchak Schneersohn, 1880–1950:** Chasidic rebbe, prolific writer, and Jewish activist. Rabbi Yosef Yitzchak, the sixth leader

continuing to encourage Jewish observance in the 1920s, the Rebbe was arrested and sentenced to death. His sentence was later commuted to ten years of hard labor, which was then changed to exile in Kostroma, a city in the Ural Mountains, about five hundred miles southeast of his home in Petersburg (then Leningrad). He was subsequently released from that sentence, but it wasn't possible for him to stay in Russia, and a short time later he left with his family to Riga, Latvia. Upon his arrival there, he was asked how he felt at that moment after all he had been through. He replied: "If someone were to offer me a billion [rubles], I would not agree to buy one minute of future suffering—but if someone were to offer me a billion [rubles] in exchange for one minute of my past suffering, I would not sell it!"[3]

The limitations in our perspective concerning how bad something is may be due to a lack of maturity. A four-year-old who has severe allergies and needs a series of shots every month might see the injections as a terrible punishment. She might feel sick the night before and come into the doctor's office crying. The same child at fourteen has a different perspective. She isn't happy about getting the shots, but she knows that without them she'll be miserable, or even in danger. As a young woman of twenty-four,

of the Chabad movement, actively promoted Jewish religious practice in Soviet Russia and was arrested for these activities. After his release from prison and exile, he settled in Riga, Latvia, and then Warsaw, Poland, from where he fled Nazi occupation and arrived in New York in 1940. Settling in Brooklyn, Rabbi Schneersohn worked to revitalize American Jewish life. His son-in-law, Rabbi Menachem Mendel Schneerson, succeeded him as the leader of the Chabad movement.

she understands that getting allergy shots allows her to work productively and is happy that her health insurance covers them.

Another example: Think of all the children who grow up in dysfunctional families, with parents who are substance abusers, neglectful, or even abandon their children entirely. We consider these children as having had "bad" childhoods. They certainly weren't easy childhoods, that's for sure! But the adult lives of these individuals can differ enormously, depending on the makeup of their personalities, the people who mentor them as they mature, and the opportunities that come their way.

The perspectives such adults have may also be influenced by poverty, prejudice (their own and that of other people), and the education to which they had access. Any one of them may turn out to be a police detective, a gangster, a welder, a banker, a business owner, a graphic artist, or a con artist. Whatever they become as adults, though, they will still carry the imprint of the trauma from their difficult childhoods.

The key question for them is: Will they be crushed by their childhood circumstances, or will they transcend them? Will they carry those traumas as chronic burdens that are more or less manageable, or will they tap into their inner resilience and be catapulted into a life of dynamic achievement? This is the question all of us who have experienced trauma must ultimately ask ourselves.

God gives us only as many difficulties, hardships, problems, trials, challenges, and tests—these terms are interchangeable—as we can handle. As the Talmud says, "According to the strength of the camel so is the load."[4] The Midrash* adds, "God said to Moses, 'When I ask [something] of them, I do not ask that they achieve it in accordance with My capacity, but in accordance with their capacity.'"[5] Does this mean that a weaker person who is less capable of managing challenges will have fewer of them, or suffer less from them? Perhaps. The weaker person might be tested with fewer and smaller challenges, but because she has a lower tolerance level, she could be equally traumatized.

Some readers may be skeptical of this notion. The idea that God only gives us difficulties that we can handle doesn't necessarily match our life experience. We can all think of individuals who were emotionally crushed by a trauma or tragedy. They may have limped through life emotionally, but they never "handled" their loss with any degree of true acceptance. This is a complex and nuanced concept that we will unpack further as this chapter and the coming chapters unfold. Stay tuned!

One idea to consider is that God has endowed humanity with Divine guidance, rules, and philosophy. He has provided the tools for spiritual connection and support. Unfortunately, many people lack those tools and have not been taught the Divine guidance and philosophy that could be psychologically lifesaving for them. In the rush toward secularism, millions of people dropped their reli-

---

* **Midrash**: The designation of a particular genre of rabbinic literature usually forming a running commentary on specific books of the Bible. The term Midrash is derived from the root of the Hebrew word *d-r-sh*, which means to search, to examine, and to investigate.

gious foundations, thinking those religious notions were antiquated and irrelevant. But during a time of crisis, they can be left foundering. Their ship is sinking, but they heedlessly punctured a hole in their life jackets.

They blame God for the crisis, but really, the fault lies with those authority figures—parents, religious teachers, other leaders, and even friends and acquaintances—who had known these fundamental religious precepts but failed to transmit them or, worse, summarily dismissed them. In failing to pass along the keys to spiritual survival during such a crisis, they are akin to parents and teachers who fail to teach children essential rules about proper nutrition and health and then wonder why their teens become obese, smokers, or both. God is the source of our Divine guidance, but God's management style is not to actively intervene. He relies on people in society to pass along these precious teachings. When we fail in that mission, widespread misery results.

If we can open ourselves to the idea that one's challenges are purposefully orchestrated by God, ultimately "*for* us, not *to* us," as is often heard in Twelve-Step teachings—even when we are in pain that clouds our ability to always clearly understand and feel this—we can feel encouraged to find and develop our inner strength. That would empower us to bear what we have been dealt, confident that, ultimately, we have the strength to carry on.

In horse racing, the stronger horses are given a small amount of extra weight to carry so the competition with the weaker horses is fairer. That's called a handicap. In human terms, this might mean that a person who demonstrates resilience and psychological strength might be expected to handle extra setbacks. In the next race of life that you run, you may be given a greater weight to bear, but even if that is the case, you can be the winner, no matter what the handicap is.

God wants your life to be as meaningful as possible, and because you're a stronger person, you may have to shoulder more issues than a less resilient person. Knowing that God has full faith in your abilities and that He wants you to live life to its fullest will help you accept your larger share of the tests and challenges that He sends you.

And God tested Abraham.[6] The thirteenth-century commentator and philosopher Rabbi Moshe ben Nachman, known as Nachmanides,∗ asks: Why did God have to put Abraham through this? Didn't He know that Abraham would come through with flying colors? Nachmanides answers that these tests were actually for Abraham's sake. Abraham was the one who needed to realize his potential, to bring that potential into actuality. The Midrash[7] gives the analogy of a potter selling earthenware. In order to show the durability of his wares to buyers, the potter kicks the pots. But he knows his wares well and only kicks the ones he knows can withstand the trauma. He studiously avoids kicking those that he knows might break.

∗ **Rabbi Moshe ben Nachman (Nachmanides, Ramban) 1194–1270:** Scholar, philosopher, author, and physician. Nachmanides was born in Spain and served as leader of Iberian Jewry. In 1263, he was summoned by King James of Aragon to a public disputation with Pablo Cristiani, a Jewish apostate. Though Nachmanides was the clear victor of the debate, he had to flee Spain because of the resulting persecution. He moved to Israel and helped reestablish communal life in Jerusalem. He authored a classic commentary on the Torah and a commentary on the Talmud.

Is there a message here for me?

You might ask, "Is the challenge a bad thing but for a good purpose, or is the challenge inherently good?" If you have the big picture in mind, it is inherently good. But most of us don't have the big picture—we all have limited perspectives and have to search to try to find the good even in the bad. Generally, the Talmud tells us, "When a person sees that he is being afflicted, he should examine his ways."[8]

We won't always get to see the "why," which depends on the event, its magnitude, and how personal it is. Yet there is always something that we can learn from a negative event. The Baal Shem Tov,* the founder of the Chasidic movement, lived in eighteenth-century Poland. He taught:[9] "In everything that a person sees or hears, there is a positive lesson for him in his service of God." Otherwise, it wouldn't have been brought to their attention.

Whether we are facing a really big issue or a smaller one that hits close to home, we have an obligation to ourselves to try to figure out what its message for us might be. Sometimes you can figure it out on your own. Other times you may need the help of an outsider who is more objective and brings a broader perspective. This is one of the reasons the Talmudic Sages advised,[10] "Provide yourself a teacher and acquire for yourself a friend."

This is one of the problems with Rabbi Kushner's posi-

---

* **Rabbi Yisrael Baal Shem Tov (Besht), 1698–1760**: Founder of the Chasidic movement. Born in Slutsk, Belarus, the Baal Shem Tov was orphaned as a child. He served as a teacher's assistant and clay digger before founding the Chasidic movement and revolutionizing the Jewish world with his emphasis on prayer, joy, and love for every Jew, regardless of his or her level of Torah knowledge.

tion that the existence of evil compromises God's power. When you need the help of someone who has a broader outlook on tragedy than yours, no one sees the big picture better than God does. In Psalms,[11] God asserts, *When he [the one suffering] calls Me, I will answer him; I am with him in his trouble.* Instead of taking this message to heart, Rabbi Kushner experienced himself as an isolated, lonely victim, even as God was sitting beside him, ready to embrace him and provide a loving shoulder on which to cry and be comforted. Rabbi Kushner's challenge was to recognize that God's omnipotence, omniscience, and all-encompassing benevolence extended to and included both his son Aaron's journey and his own. In his pain, the rabbi locked God out.

None of this makes understanding or accepting tragedy or harsh circumstances easy. We may struggle to get a proper handle on a tragic event and end up concluding, perhaps rightfully, "Really, there is no way that a human being can comprehend the significance of this event." That is fair. And yet, I believe we still have a responsibility to follow that up with, "Fine. We may not understand it today, but we can accept that there is more to the human experience than the here and now."

Brigadier General Ran Ronen-Pekker of the Israeli Air Force was considered by one of his pilots to be "the greatest squadron commander ever." He defended Israel in several wars and was the commander of the Tel Nof Airbase. He once had a long audience with the Lubavitcher Rebbe, Rabbi Menachem Mendel Schneerson.* The fol-

---

* **Rabbi Menachem Mendel Schneerson, 1902–1994:** The towering

lowing is an excerpt from the Brigadier General's notes of that meeting:

> At one point, the Rebbe suggested that I begin putting on tefillin.*
>
> I said, "Though I am a believer, I'm not a religious man, and tefillin do not mean very much to me."
>
> He asked me: "Do you not believe in God?"
>
> "Let me tell you about God," I responded, and I told him about my friend since childhood, Zorik Lev.
>
> I told of the tragedy of Zorik, who was killed in the '73 [Yom Kippur] War, and Udi, his fifteen-year-old son who died two years later in his mother's arms from an asthma attack. I asked the rabbi, "Where is God, and if He exists, why is He so cruel to this family? Why doesn't God divide up the suffering?"
>
> I insisted that he address the incident and admit that it was particularly horrific. At first, he tried to avoid a direct response, but in the end he acknowledged that, indeed, the episode was difficult and appalling.
>
> He said, "We are mere mortals; who are we to judge God's actions? I am only seventy-three, and I learn

---

Jewish leader of the twentieth century, known as the Lubavitcher Rebbe, or simply as the Rebbe. Born in southern Ukraine, the Rebbe escaped Nazi-occupied Europe, arriving in the US in June 1941. The Rebbe inspired and guided the revival of traditional Judaism after the European devastation, impacting virtually every Jewish community the world over. The Rebbe often emphasized that the performance of just one additional good deed could usher in the era of Mashiach. The Rebbe's scholarly talks and writings have been printed in more than two hundred volumes.

* Small leather boxes worn on the head and on the arm next to the heart during weekday morning prayers. The boxes contain biblical verses written by a scribe on parchment.

more and become wiser every day, while God is eternal and much smarter than all of us. One cannot judge things only by the present; one must see the whole picture, including past and future. Perhaps the deaths of Zorik and Udi saved or will save the lives of many others."

He saw that the explanation did not satisfy me and returned to the subject several times during the conversation.[12]

The Rebbe was one of the wisest men of our generation, yet even with his staggering level of knowledge and wisdom, he could not offer a definitive response about the reasons for a specific tragedy. The Rebbe affirmed that there is more to human existence and what happens to us than the here and now. There's also a before and an after. Life's mysteries, including its tragedies, often defy full understanding while we are still in the here and now.

We do know that each soul comes into this world for a purpose, and the soul also lives on after the body's death.* It may go on to heaven and even go through another incarnation. Life in this physical world is just one part of an individual's total existence. Within our limited frame of reference during this lifetime, the pains and losses we suffer may be doubly painful because we can't see the reasons for them ... so, we perceive them as bad.

This may be a new and difficult concept for many people. What we can see and understand in this lifetime is very limited. Much more will be revealed in the Afterlife. Our lifespan of seventy, eighty, or even ninety or more

---

* Discussed in more detail in Chapter 9.

years simply cannot be the be-all and end-all of our existence, because there's too much injustice that is not rectified in this world. And because God is good, it must be reconciled in the Afterlife.

Even if we believe in God and His goodness completely, we might try to content ourselves by saying, "This situation is beyond my comprehension. If I had the whole picture, which includes what will happen to the soul in the hereafter, perhaps then I could understand." Or we might then be able to say with confidence, "Yes, there *is* rhyme and reason somewhere."

Only God knows the real reasons for the events He orchestrates in this life. Our souls intuitively understand that God sees the big picture that we can't see. During the next stage of our journey, when our souls are in the Afterlife, we will enjoy an expanded perspective. Only then can we begin to understand what took place while we were here in this world. For now, with our limitations, we must turn to and rely on God.

The prophet Isaiah[13] assures us, *You [the Jewish people] will say on that day [when Mashiach arrives], "I thank You, God, for You were angry with me. And now Your wrath has subsided, and You have comforted me."*

God is waiting for us to alleviate suffering

Our comfort and reassurance grow when we cultivate an acceptance that all our problems—even those that threaten to completely overwhelm us—are not necessarily absolutely "bad," because, ultimately, they come from God, and God is good. Cultivating this mindset takes practice.

Similarly, it will be helpful for us to notice our feelings of resentment, anger, or disillusionment with God, and then accept them without judgment. But after we have gained that foothold on acceptance, we need to know that there is a higher level we can achieve. This higher level is understanding that there is much we cannot understand. The question of "Why?" can continue to haunt us without leading to any satisfying answers. The "why" question is ultimately not helpful. Climbing the rungs to higher stages of acceptance *is* helpful.

There is another compelling reason that we don't—and *shouldn't*—have an answer to the question of why people suffer.

In a public talk,[14] the Lubavitcher Rebbe spoke about the suffering in the world, and when he came to these words, he began to sob:

> *If He is capable of anything,*
> *why can't He provide good without the bad?*
> *And if His Torah answers all questions, why does it not*
> *answer this?*
>
> *There can be only one answer:*
>
> *He does not wish us to know,*
> *because if we knew,*
> *we might consent*
> *and let such a world be.*

Building on this response, Rabbi Lord Jonathan Sacks,*

* **Rabbi Lord Jonathan Sacks, 1948–2020,** was known as an international religious leader, philosopher, and respected moral voice. The chief rabbi of the UK and the Commonwealth from 1991 to 2013 and the recipient of the 2016 Templeton Prize, he was the award-winning author of over

former chief rabbi of the United Kingdom and considered one of the twenty-first century's greatest ambassadors for Orthodox Judaism, said that the religious question in the face of disaster is not, "Why did this happen?"; rather, it is, "What then shall we do?" The appropriate response, Rabbi Sacks said, "is not to seek to understand, thereby to accept. We are not God. Instead, we are the people He has called on to be his partners in the work of creation."[15]

Rabbi Aron Moss,* a teacher, author, and congregational rabbi in Sydney, Australia, explained why a satisfying explanation is ill-advised:

> If this ultimate question were answered, then we would be able to make peace with the suffering of innocents, and that is unthinkable.... We would no longer be bothered by their cry, we would no longer feel their pain, because we would understand why it is happening....
>
> And so, if we could make sense of innocent people suffering, if we could rationalize tragedy, then we could live with it. We would be able to hear the cry of sweet children in pain and not be horrified. We would tolerate seeing broken hearts and shattered lives, for we would

---

thirty-five books, including *Not in God's Name* and *Morality: Restoring the Common Good in Divided Times.* A frequent and sought-after contributor to radio, television, and the international press, and a renowned public speaker, Rabbi Sacks was awarded degrees from both Cambridge and Oxford Universities and was granted nineteen honorary degrees from universities around the world. He was knighted by Her Majesty, the Queen in 2005 and took his seat in the House of Lords in October 2009.

* **Rabbi Aron Moss:** Rabbi and author. Rabbi Moss is a teacher of Kabbalah, Talmud, and practical Judaism in Sydney, Australia. He serves as rabbi of the Nefesh Synagogue and authors a popular weekly syndicated article on modern Jewish thought.

be able to neatly explain them away. Our question would be answered, and we could move on.

But as long as the pain of innocents remains a burning question, we are bothered by its existence. As long as we can't explain pain, we must alleviate it. If innocent people suffering does not fit into our worldview, we must eradicate it. Rather than justifying their pain, we need to get rid of it... .

Start formulating a response... . When you see innocent people suffering, help them. Combat the pain in the world with goodness. Alleviate suffering wherever you can... . [W]e dare not leave it up to God to alleviate suffering. He is waiting for us to do it. That's what we are here for.[16]

"I prefer to be down here with the questions rather than up there with the answers"

We again turn to Rabbi Lord Jonathan Sacks, who discusses a truly exemplary individual's instructive response to extreme and traumatic loss:

I heard of a rabbi [the Klausenberger Rebbe, Rabbi Yekusiel Yehudah Halberstam (10 January 1905–18 June 1994)] who went through the Holocaust and lost his wife and all eleven children and was asked afterward, "Do you have no questions of God?"

He replied, "Of course I have questions of God. My questions of God are so powerful that were I to ask them, God Himself would invite me up to heaven to give me the answers. And I prefer to be down here on earth with the questions than up there in heaven with the answers."

*Now, that sounds clever, but actually it's very profound.
I have said many times, faith is not certainty. Faith is
the courage to live with uncertainty. After the Holocaust, uncertainty is where we live.*[17]

That is a very Jewish reply. If we found an argument
that satisfied us as to why bad things happen to good
people, we would be reconciled with bad things happening to good people. Since we have only the question and
not the answer, therefore, we work tirelessly so that bad
things do not continue to happen to good people. We con-
duct medical research to prevent or cure disease. We become trained as first responders so we can race to scenes
of crimes, accidents, or disasters to render aid. We speak
out, write, and march against injustice. Sometimes faith
lies in the question and the need to make a difference, not
in the answer.

Rabbi Tzvi Freeman, senior editor at Chabad.org and
author of several books, takes this argument a step further. He calls on Jews to struggle against suffering that
some might accept as God's will:

*When you see a person suffering, you don't say, "God
runs the universe. God will take care of it. God knows
what is best." You do everything in your power to relieve
that suffering as though there is no God. You become a
heretic in God's name.*[18]

This brings us full circle to the question in the title of
this chapter: What is evil, and why does it exist? By now
I hope you'll agree that we have defined evil as *that which
opposes the will of God.* God *Himself,* by His own volition,
as part of His master plan, created the option of evil and

implanted it in humans. But God gave us all free choice. He left it up to us, to humankind, to choose to commit acts of evil or to choose to commit acts of goodness. God created evil, but He does not cause human beings to wield it.

It's our choice: We can cling to our instinctive selfishness that crosses into evil, opposing God's will. Or we can choose the good and act as His partner in making our world a place of goodness and peace.

Chapter Summary: *If bad things never happened in the world, we would be good from birth, but that goodness would be passive, automatic, unchallenged, unearned, and ultimately meaningless. If we did not experience evil, we wouldn't be able to recognize the need for good and would never learn how to be good. We would have no heroes, because heroism would not be necessary. When we work against evil, we become God's partner in making the world a place of goodness and peace.*

Endnotes:

1   Deuteronomy 13:5; 28:9.
2   *Shabbat* 133b; *Sotah* 14a.
3   *Sefer Hasichot* 5688–5691 (Brooklyn, NY: Kehot Publication Society, 1995), Introduction.
4   *Ketubot* 67a.
5   *Bamidbar Rabbah* 12:3; *Tanchuma Naso* 11.
6   Genesis 22:1.
7   *Bereishit Rabbah* 32:3.
8   *Brachot* 5a.
9   *Sefer Hasichot Kayitz* 5700 (Brooklyn, NY: Kehot Publication Society, 1947).
10   *Avot* 1:6.
11   Psalms 91:15.
12   Interview with Brigadier General Ran Ronen-Pekker, "The View from Fifty Thousand Feet," from *My Story,* Vol. 1 (Brooklyn, NY: Jewish Educational Media, 2017).
13   Isaiah 12:1.
14   Unedited talk, Hoshana Rabbah, 1983.
15   Rabbi Lord Jonathan Sacks, "Why Does God Allow Terrible Things to Happen to His People?" *The Times of London*, January 1, 2005.
16   Rabbi Aron Moss, "Why Do Bad Things Happen to Good People?" Chabad.org.
17   Rabbi Lord Jonathan Sacks, "Rabbi Sacks on the Holocaust – A project for Yom HaShoah in partnership with the Holocaust Educational Trust, Topic 3: Jewish Theology and the Holocaust," transcript, part 1. rabbisacks.org.
18   Rabbi Tzvi Freeman, "Heresy in God's Name," Chabad.org.

CHAPTER FOUR

Is There Really a God?

An atheist is walking through the forest when Big Foot jumps out at him. The atheist yells, "God, help me!" A second later, a voice rumbles from heaven, "I thought you didn't believe in Me." "Well," the man says, "until a minute ago I didn't believe in Big Foot, either."

People often ask me whether God exists.

The short answer is yes.

The long answer is ... a little more complicated.

It's understandable that people have difficulty getting a grasp on God, because God is beyond any conception. Although God created the natural world and many think of Him as present within nature, traditional Jewish thinkers do not consider God to be part of nature. God is *in* the world but not *of* the world. Likewise, the Bible speaks of God in human terms, making references to God's features, such as face, back, arm, hand, and voice, yet these words are anthropomorphic and allegorical.

Many of us bring a childhood image of God into our adult years. We still envision an old man with a long white beard (perhaps based on Daniel's vision[1]) sitting on a majestic throne.* The Jewish view of God is not a physical,

---

* *I watched as thrones were set up, and the One of Ancient Days [God] sat.*

material, or human form. To help us relate to God, we assign many roles to Him in our liturgy—Father, King, Rock, and Shepherd, to name just a few—but we see these roles metaphorically. They help us understand aspects of God's various personas interacting with us in this world.

My goal here is not to prove that there is a God—that task is futile. God's existence cannot be proven, but, I hasten to add, neither can it be disproven. Keep in mind, too, that atheism—the belief that there is no God—is also an act of faith: the nonexistence of God cannot be proven and, in fact, may be harder to prove than the existence of God.

In my experience as a rabbi and teacher, a primary sticking point for people concerning the existence of God is simply their inexperience with God. It's not so much that they *don't* believe in God; it's that they have no frame of reference for what belief in God might mean. Furthermore, if they believed in God, they might be unsure of how to recognize what they are supposed to feel.

A secondary point is that many people have a built-in bias against believing in God. In a way, this is understandable. Who in their right mind wants to be burdened by an all-knowing and all-seeing Boss Who keeps strict moral standards, with penalties for violations of the code? It could be so guilt-inducing that some could reject it out of hand!

Even many scientists who study the origins of the universe struggle with this, too. While we like to think of

---

His garment was white as snow, and the hair on His head like clean wool; His throne was of fiery flames, its wheels blazing fire.

scientists as the ultimate truth-seekers, cultural, academic, financial, and even political biases may seep into their work and cloud their results. Whether consciously or unwittingly, some begin their research with the conclusion they want to reach, and only then do they seek evidence that will support it. Scientists who didn't believe in the existence of God but continued to find mounting evidence for it, particularly relating to the origins of the universe, have found these discoveries particularly vexing. In *God and the Astronomers,* Dr. Robert Jastrow, world-renowned astrophysicist, describes the astronomical discoveries of recent years and the theological implications of the new insights afforded by science into mankind's place in the cosmos. He explains the chain of events that forced astronomers, despite their initial reluctance— "'Irritating,' said Einstein; 'Repugnant,' said the great British astronomer Eddington; 'I would like to reject it,' said MIT physicist Philip Morrison"[2]—to accept the validity of the Big Bang and the fact that the universe began in a moment of creation.

Therefore, it's no wonder that, rather than posit a deity, many scientists would conjure up their own unprovable theories about the origins of the universe (or, more accurately, the hypothetical multiverse). None of this "science" disproves the existence of God.

Many people who were initially ambivalent about a belief in God still appreciated and sought out Jewish learning. The brilliant Torah scholar Rabbi Adin Even-Israel Steinsaltz,* prolific author of over sixty books and an Is-

---

* **Rabbi Adin Even-Israel (Steinsaltz), 1937–2020:** Talmudist, author,

rael Prize laureate, grew up in Israel in a secular family
that believed in communism. Concerning the Torah education he received as a child, Steinsaltz explains:

> When I was ten years old, my father hired a private Tal-
> mud teacher for me. His name was Professor Epstein,
> and we studied bareheaded (without the traditional
> Jewish head covering).

> My father told me, "If you will become an atheist, that
> doesn't bother me. I'm an atheist. But I do not want
> that a child in our family should be an am haaretz—an
> ignoramus [Jewishly]."[3]

Is your conception of God stuck in a time warp?

Often, those who were introduced to God as children in a
Hebrew school or Sunday school environment—but never had the opportunity to deepen their understanding of
Him—find it hard to believe in and connect to Him. While
the rest of their personality and education will have ma-
tured and grown more sophisticated, their image of God
might remain in a time warp—frozen in the understanding of an eight-year-old. With no follow-up in religious
education past the age of twelve or thirteen, this stunted
view can result in their dismissing religious people's be-

---

and philosopher. Rabbi Even-Israel (Steinsaltz) is considered one of the
foremost Jewish thinkers of the twentieth century. A resident of Jerusalem, Rabbi Steinsaltz was the founder of the Israel Institute for Talmudic
Publications, a society dedicated to the translation and elucidation of the
Talmud, and he authored numerous works about the Talmud and Jewish
mysticism. Praised by *Time* magazine as a "once-in-a-millennium scholar,"
he was awarded the Israel Prize for his contributions to Jewish study.

liefs as simplistic, backward, or superstitious, out of sync with today's "real" world.

Nothing can be further from the truth. Monotheistic religion has a storied and hallowed past, with a depth and character that match and surpass other great philosophies. However, for many people, the huge emptiness where their religious education should have been in their formative years creates a seemingly unbridgeable chasm between disbelief and belief. For the uninitiated or only minimally educated, religion can seem like an unreliable and even useless crutch. They cannot know the depth, profundity, and meaning inherent in a religious life. For the religious, faith in God is a solid foundation on which one can build a purposeful life.

"Is it absurd to look for God? It is just as absurd not to look for Him."

In his classic, bestselling introduction to Judaism entitled *This Is My God,* novelist Herman Wouk talks about the things that can lead Jews adrift: lack of training, lack of will, sharp changes of environment, persecution, absorbing interests, and intellectual alienation. The reason most people give is almost always the last—intellectual alienation. But, he adds, most people lose their feeling of positive Jewish identity because they never had a chance to find it.

Wouk describes the process by which he became an observant Jew as a young man:

> *I was gambling my whole existence on one hunch: that being a Jew was not a trivial and somewhat inconve-*

*nient accident, but the best thing in my life; that to be
a Jew the soundest way was the classic way. I took the
chance, saying to myself, "I may be wrong." Living this
way on a gamble, I learned things about Judaism that
no other procedure could have taught me. The faith
would have remained a closed book to me—except as
childhood nostalgia—had I not made the experiment.
There are many things that you can come to know only
by trying to do them... .*

*Is it absurd to look for God? It is just as absurd not to
look for Him, life today being what it is. No one can
make the decision except out of the impulse of his heart,
but he can make it without taking leave of his senses or
his critical intelligence. It may be, quite the other way,
that his critical intelligence will force the decision.*[4]

How Judaism was born

Judaism is the parent religion of Christianity and Islam
and was born in the Sinai Desert some three thousand,
three hundred years ago. Just seven weeks after their Exodus from Egypt, the descendants of Abraham, Isaac, and
Jacob encountered God at the foot of Mount Sinai, where
they camped and waited while their leader Moses went
up to the mountaintop to receive the Ten Commandments—the foundation for Jewish living.

In a cataclysmic event, including thunder, lightning,
and the mountain on fire, this nomadic people—so recently slaves—heard God announcing to them, *I am the
Lord, your God, Who has taken you out of the land of Egypt!*
This was followed by nine additional declarations or commandments. From that moment on, every person present

formed the nucleus of the Jewish nation. They experienced the giving of the Law en masse and, based on a covenant with God, passed down this history-changing event to their descendants, from generation to generation, in an unbroken living tradition to this day.

The revelation at Mount Sinai became the epic and defining event of their lives. The revelation was also documented in detail in the Torah, which forms the basis for Jewish history and law. Today, Jews observe a tradition derived from that history and law given by God through Moses. Eventually, the written law integrated with an oral tradition that has also been passed down through the generations.

The supernatural aspect of so many of God's acts can strike people as incredible and unprovable. "The ten plagues, the splitting of the Sea of Reeds, the manna descending from heaven, water flowing like a well out of a rock: How are we supposed to believe anyone can do those things?" they ask. "These can't be proven scientifically! Are we supposed to consider God great and holy because of His ability to do a few magic tricks?"

Maimonides was concerned about this perception more than eight hundred years ago. He labored for ten years on his magnum opus, the code of Jewish law, *Mishneh Torah* ("The Torah Reviewed"), written in a lucid Hebrew style. The code offers a brilliant systemization of all of Jewish law and doctrine, and it includes a discussion about this specific theological sticking point:

> *The Jews did not believe in Moses our teacher—and by extension, God—because of the wonders that he per-*

formed. Whenever anyone's belief is based on wonders, his commitment is flawed, because it is possible to per-form a wonder through magic or sorcery.

What is the source of our belief in Him? The revelation at Mount Sinai. Our eyes saw, and not a stranger's. Our ears heard, and not another's. There was fire, thunder, and lightning. Moses entered the thick clouds; the Voice spoke to him, and we heard, "Moses, Moses, go tell them the following... ."

Thus, the Torah[5] relates: Face to face, God spoke to you, *and* God did not make this covenant with our fathers [but with us, who are all here alive today].[6] *How is it known that the revelation at Mount Sinai alone is proof of the truth of Moses' prophecy that leaves no shortcoming? As it is stated[7]:* Behold, I will come to you in a thick cloud so that the people will hear Me speaking to you and will believe in you—Moses—for-ever. *It appears that before this [the revelation at Sinai] happened, they did not believe in him with a faith that would last forever; rather, it was with a faith that al-lowed for suspicions and doubts.[8]*

This revelation was not something *told* to them. It was *experienced* communally by an entire nation, two million people, and they passed it on from father to son and from mother to daughter, for over three thousand, three hundred years.

Now, while some might argue that Moses used the same sound-effects crew as Paramount Pictures did in the 1956 epic film *The Ten Commandments,* Jews believe that the revelation was the only time that heaven and earth and God and man met face to face, as it were. Moses returned to his people forty days later with two stone tablets on which the Ten Commandments were engraved.

Therefore, we see that both the Jewish nation and the Jewish religion were established from a vast communal experience. In contrast, Christianity, Islam, and the majority of other religions were based on the premise that God revealed Himself to an individual. These claims of a personal revelation to an individual cannot be proved or disproved.

The documented claim that two million people all experienced communal revelation would not stand uncontested unless it were true. If it hadn't happened, surely those who had been there would have risen up to dispute the claim, saying, "That's not how it happened!" They would offer counterevidence that this extraordinary event never took place. This is certain because they were a cantankerous, stiff-necked, and rebellious people who tested Moses' leadership ten times[9] throughout their journey in the desert. A people this driven to questioning, quarrelling, and complaining would absolutely have denied the revelation.

Another obstacle to belief in God is that people often reject what they don't understand. As we explored in the previous chapter, many people cannot accept the idea that God is all-good *and* all-powerful while also accepting that evil exists in the world. The two ideas appear to be in total conflict. From their vantage point, if God does not prevent bad things from happening to individual people or to groups of people, they conclude that the God they were taught about as children doesn't operate as a Presence in the world today. They also do not find the "big picture" idea credible or satisfying—that what appears and feels bad today has meaning and purpose that only God can understand but is invisible to us. Eventually, when the full story has unfolded to reveal its purpose as God intended, *that* is when we can see, in retrospect, the meaning and purpose that we could not see earlier. Ultimately, then, these painful events can be seen as having been for the good.

Here is an example of this, straight from the Torah: Joseph, Jacob's son, was sold into slavery by his ten brothers when he was seventeen years old. After languishing in an Egyptian prison for twelve years, he became viceroy of Egypt at the age of thirty. Nine years later, Joseph's family, including his elderly father, settled in the area of Goshen, Egypt, to escape the famine that had afflicted their homeland, Canaan.

Years later, when Jacob died, the brothers worried that Joseph, still Egypt's viceroy, would now avenge their mistreatment of him, even though Joseph had already assured them that he harbored them no ill will. Joseph understood clearly that it was God's will that he be somehow brought to Egypt and experience all that he did there, eventually becoming the viceroy. Ultimately, his brothers' involvement in this scenario (including selling him as a slave) was part of God's way of fulfilling His plan for all the involved parties—including protecting Joseph's family, along with the entire region, from famine.

Still insecure about Joseph's true feelings, the brothers told him that their father made a deathbed request that

Joseph should fully forgive them for orchestrating his sale as a slave. Joseph's response reiterated what he had told them earlier: *Do not be afraid. Shall I take God's place? You might have meant to do me harm. However, God meant for it to be for the good, where the lives of multitudes have been saved [from the famine].*[10]

When I hear people challenge the existence of God because they do not seem to understand Him, I show them that they unquestioningly accept many realities that they do not understand. I ask, "Do you understand what electricity is and how it works? How about the laws of gravity? Can you explain how computers and their software are able to do thousands of things that seem supernatural to the layperson?"

Even when some people shrug and answer generically, "That's just how it is," or "It's just nature" to a great variety of mystifying questions, that is no answer at all. "Nature" is simply a word used for phenomena that defy quick or easy explanations or understanding. But even when we don't understand the inner workings of many phenomena, we still manage to believe that they exist.

You can drive from point A to point B even if you "don't believe in carburetors"

Some readers of this book who work in the fields of computer science and artificial intelligence undoubtedly consider answers to these questions elementary. But most of us are not knowledgeable about how computers work, and we're fascinated by what they can do. Computers can perform tasks in nanoseconds, such as solving complex mathematical problems or compiling and organizing enormous amounts of information from myriad different sources. Calculations that used to require the labor of several people over many months can now be completed in seconds. We can lock our doors, do our banking, order goods, and plan intercontinental travel through our phones, which are also powerful computers.

Who would have thought, not so many years ago, that hundreds of millions of us would carry devices in our pockets—or on our wrists!—that can take stunning photographs, record high quality voice and video, perform math calculations, communicate in a hundred different formats, play music, provide weather reports, and serve up the latest news? To most of us, those capabilities are mind-boggling and magical—you might even say God-like.

By and large, the same people who say they can't understand God have no idea how carburetors work, and yet, their cars drive just fine, and the world keeps turning, too. How? We don't know. But you can drive from point A to point B even if you "don't believe in carburetors" or understand them, or even if you doubt their very existence!

If machines designed and made by mere humans can do magical, inexplicable things, why shouldn't God? If a huge bank of servers can store data on billions of people and operate the world's infrastructure, then why shouldn't God be able to calculate and evaluate everyone's good and bad deeds between Rosh Hashanah and Yom Kippur? It was God Who endowed human beings with the gift of intelligence and the creativity to fashion literature, art, and music. Why shouldn't we believe that He has powers that are at least similar to those of the cyber-scientists with their amazing hardware and software?

King David referred to this in his own way:[11]

> *Understand, you senseless among the people;*
> *fools, when will you become wise?*
>
> *Shall He Who implants the ear not hear? Shall He Who*
> *forms the eye not see?*
>
> *He Who imparts knowledge to man [shall he not know]?*

We depend on technology to run our world smoothly—whether we understand its operating system or not. Likewise, we have always needed to rely on God, whether or not we understand how He works.

The disciples of the Maggid of Mezritch,* an early Chasidic leader, once pondered the question, "If I were God, how would I have created the world?" Rabbi Levi Yitzchak of Berditchev said, "I would have made a more improved world in this way." Another said, "I would have made a more improved world in another way." But one of the Maggid's students, Rabbi Schneur Zalman of Liadi,** who became the first leader of Chabad, disagreed with

---

* **Rabbi Dov Ber of Mezritch, d. 1772:** Primary disciple and eventual successor of the Baal Shem Tov, known as "the Maggid of Mezritch." Among his disciples were the founders of various Chasidic dynasties, including Rabbi Nachum of Chernobyl, Rabbi Levi Yitzchak of Berditchev, and Rabbi Schneur Zalman of Liadi. His teachings, recorded by his students, appear in various volumes, including *Maggid Devarav L'Yaakov.*

** **Rabbi Schneur Zalman of Liadi (Alter Rebbe), 1745–1812:** Chasidic rebbe, halachic authority, and founder of the Chabad movement. The Alter Rebbe was born in Liozna, Belarus, and was among the principal students of the Maggid of Mezritch. His numerous works include the *Tanya,* an early classic containing the fundamentals of Chabad Chasidism; and *Shulchan Aruch Harav,* an expanded and reworked code of Jewish law.

them on what *they* said they would do. He said: "If you were God, you would make the world exactly the way God made it, because God is perfect, and if He made the world this way, obviously this is the perfect world."

People who are uncomfortable with the existence of God often feel threatened or challenged by the idea that God runs the world. They resent the idea that He's the One in charge and that everyone's life is unfolding according to the Divine will. "Don't we have free will?" they ask. "Aren't we more than puppets with God pulling our strings?" If God is omnipotent and omniscient—the Big Boss, with 24/7 surveillance—then where does our self-determination fit in?"

It is axiomatic in the Torah that we have both free will and control in certain areas, most obviously over the moral and religious issues that we confront in life. These types of issues come up constantly. Some are matters of life and death, such as whether and when we may pull the plug on a moribund relative. Others are more pedestrian, such as whether we should keep the accidental overpayment from a client and hope she doesn't ever notice, or inform her and refund the difference. Or whether to share the bit of juicy gossip you just heard about a mutual friend or keep it to yourself. These are moral and ethical decisions that we face all the time. This is where we exercise our true free will.

We have no choice, however, regarding when, where, and to whom we will be born, in what circumstances, and how we will be raised, even though these factors profoundly affect who we will become. These were all planned by God without any input from us. In virtually everything else—outside of our free will to make moral, spiritual, and religious decisions—the outcome of everything we do is also in God's hands. God also decides when and whether we are granted specific opportunities or challenges, whether we need a punishment or wake-up call of some kind, or whether we should be forgiven for a wrong action. God also decides how long we will live.

A life-saving bullet in the jaw

Here's an example: If you walk across the street against the light in front of a truck, and God's will is that you won't be killed, it probably isn't because the cars part around you like the Sea of Reeds or that God lifts you like a flying bird and you fly over the traffic. What will probably happen is the truck will hit you and you'll be grievously injured. Then you'll be in a hospital, and hopefully you will meditate about the recklessness of what you did. Stepping in front of the truck was not only foolish, but it also violates our moral and religious responsibility to preserve and protect our physical health. Specifically, crossing the street against traffic violates God's prohibition against putting yourself in danger. And this doesn't even take into account the endangerment of the drivers who must swerve to avoid hitting you, and the horror experienced by the truck driver who had no choice but to unintentionally hit you.

Even the gunman who kills someone during a holdup is

only the unbidden volunteer to do that which God would have done anyway, because God decided that the victim's time to die had arrived. And for having volunteered for this task, *unbidden*, the criminal has taken the law into his own hands and will pay for his crime. Consider this: The one who throws the switch on the electric chair for one who was judged liable for capital punishment is an officer of the court following the law. Anyone else performing the same action, even if his intention is to be a vigilante, is guilty of murder.

Many years ago, a friend of mine in Montreal whom I'll call Saul was returning to his *yeshivah*, an institution of Torah learning for young men, after a Friday evening Shabbat meal. It was around 10 p.m. when he was confronted by a hoodlum with a gun. "Give me all your money!" the robber ordered. Saul said he didn't carry money or anything else on Shabbat, so he had nothing to give him. The would-be robber now became a would-be murderer, shooting Saul point-blank in the face before running off.

Saul was in shock, but he managed to stagger across the street to his dorm room. His roommate took one look at him, saw his bleeding face, and called an ambulance, which rushed Saul to the hospital. Saul was examined and stabilized, and then he waited for the surgeon to arrive. After the surgeon examined the X-rays and consulted some colleagues, he decided that since the bullet had lodged itself in his jaw without fracturing it, attempting to remove it would do more damage than just leaving it where it was. For more than fifty years, Saul has carried this lead and steel momento from that encounter in his jaw, a constant reminder that his time had not come on that Friday night.

This kind of story doesn't make much sense to the modern, secular thinker. The robber wasn't thinking about God when he pulled the trigger and shot Saul. He didn't plan the holdup because God told him to. He shot this young man because he wanted money and Saul didn't have any to give. The robber's intentions were evil, and he exercised his free will, choosing to rob and shoot his victim. Had he been apprehended, he would have had to stand trial and receive whatever punishment the law provided. Had the robber killed my friend Saul, he would have been the vile instrument fulfilling God's will, attesting that God had previously decided Saul's time to die *had* come. Still, that would not have mitigated the vicious robber's culpability, either morally or in the civic arena.

A few years ago, the father of a friend of mine, an eighty-eight-year-old Holocaust survivor, was walking to the synagogue for services at 6:30 in the morning. At his age and stage, he couldn't make it across the street within the time allotted by the traffic signal. Therefore, he always waited for someone else to accompany him across the street. As they crossed together, drivers waiting for the light to change noticed them, understood the need to be patient for a few more seconds, and waited until the men had safely crossed. This was a daily occurrence that was usually carried off without a hitch. One fateful day, a young man whom I know well was also rushing to the synagogue in his car, but he did not see the men concluding their crossing. Tragically, the young man hit them, throwing both pedestrians many yards. The elderly man was killed, and his acquaintance was severely injured.

The tragedy was huge, compounded by the fact that in the close-knit community, everyone knew all parties involved.

During the weeklong mourning period called *shivah*, my friend, whose elderly father had been killed, sent a message to the driver: *Our family does not harbor any ill will toward you. Do not ruin your life because of this. It was God's will.*

While this might sound outrageously generous, it is consistent with the Jewish outlook on life.

A young man, twenty-two years old, was Jet-Skiing with two friends in Miami Beach. One of the friends started roughhousing, trying to show off how close he could get to the others without hitting them ... until he hit one of them.

This twenty-two-year-old, who was hit, drowned.

His mother, who had lost her husband just five years earlier, had to bear the burden alone. In the midst of the intense *shivah* week, the two friends came to her home to offer their condolences. I cannot imagine the courage that it took for them to do so. The mother said to them, "I do not want you to ruin your lives because of this accident. I know it was God's will. You should go on with your lives." The driver of the Jet-Ski who killed her son and his friend stood there and cried. They cried for the loss of their dear friend, they cried for their role in the tragedy, they cried for this mother's aplomb and magnanimity in offering full forgiveness, and they cried for the depth of her faith.

By the way, both the driver of the car and the navigator on the Jet-Ski were exonerated by the police investigations that followed.

Can you imagine how freeing such an outlook can be, not only for the unwitting perpetrators of these tragedies but also for the survivors? If both the people who were the agents of these deaths as well as the survivors could accept this philosophy, they would not be weighed down by all the "what ifs" and "if onlys" that would have only added salt to their wounds. In these cases, I'm glad to say the survivors and the "drivers" of the events did believe and did understand that God is in charge. Some people are meant to live for eighty-eight years and die peacefully in bed. Others are destined to die violently in an accident while going to synagogue to pray to God. Some twenty-two-year-olds are just setting out in life with so much promise ahead of them; others have already completed their mission at the same age.

If God doesn't exist, no value is absolute. Life is just one big crapshoot.

The Talmud cautions against walking near an inclining wall,[12] which in our times we can equate to not walking next to a construction site with a sign that says, "DANGER!" Some of the Talmud's commentators asked, "Why aren't you allowed to go there? Isn't it true that if you're not destined to be injured, nothing will happen to you?"

The commentaries answer that when you put yourself in a dangerous situation, you are asking for the Heavenly Court to give your life a "performance review." Your merits will be measured against your misdeeds or sins. If the Heavenly Court—or God's bank of servers in his data cloud, if you will—has to evaluate your moral standing at this time, do not make it a higher stakes calculation. You would be forcing God to choose one of two options: Either He will protect you above and beyond what you deserve, or He will allow nature to have its way. That's when the readout of deeds (in your "performance review") is important. Do you have enough credits to convince the Heavenly Court to protect you? That's why the Talmud cautions against placing yourself in danger.

Although you may not be the master of your fate, you are the captain of your ship. You weren't in charge when your son started using drugs, but you are in charge of how you respond to that challenge. You can't make God or even other people behave the way you want them to, but you get to decide how you handle what life throws at you.

Faith is not something you either have or don't have. We each have a soul, which manifests as a Godly faith-instinct within ourselves. Whether we acknowledge it or deny it, it is there. Faith expresses itself in many ways. It can be an intellectual realization that springs from one's upbringing and experience. It can express itself through one's emotions, whether passionate or subdued. Or it can be like a seed, planted but not yet germinated.

Even people most distant from God may seek Him in moments of great need. Think of the times when a troubled person says, "God, I'm not a praying man, but please help me out here." A cynic may sneer at a death-row conversion as an evil person hedging his bets, but there's a lot of truth in the adage, "There are no atheists in foxholes." The person facing a moment of truth may well be experiencing a sincere recognition of what he neglected in life.

A father was walking with his young son in a crowded shopping mall when suddenly his son disappeared, swept up among the sea of holiday shoppers. The father ran this way and that, trying desperately to locate his son, to no avail. Finally, he said, "God, You know I never ask You for anything, but if You give me my son back, I'll do anything for You."

A moment later, the boy came wandering down the hallway, completely unaware of the havoc he had caused by disappearing. The father looked up at God and said, "It's okay, God. He's here. Never mind."

Right!?

The Previous Lubavitcher Rebbe, Rabbi Yosef Yitzchak Schneersohn, was in Warsaw, Poland, in September 1939 while it was under German aerial bombing. The bombardment was ferocious, relentless. Multi-story buildings collapsed. Street after street of houses were going up in flames, and clusters of smoking black clouds burst out of the windows, shutting out the light of what had naturally been a fine sunny day. The Rebbe and many others kept running from one shelter to another, exhausted but trying to remain alive.

The following is an excerpt from a translation of what the Rebbe, who referred to the horrors of that day as "indescribable" and one of the most difficult days of his life, wrote about it:

*In one of those havens [shelters], a few hundred people
of various stripes had assembled. Jews with long coats,
beards, and* peyos *(sidelocks), and women wearing wigs;
clean-shaven Jews, and women who spoke only Polish—
all stood there, cowed and vexed.*

*Our group—myself and my family, and a few dozen stu-
dents of* Tomchei Temimim, *the rabbinical seminary—
said* Tehillim *[Psalms]. Suddenly there was a fearsome
blast: a bomb exploded near our group. A river of fire
immediately gushed forth. Every one of us saw death
before his eyes.*

*And at that very moment, everyone cried out in one
voice:* Shema Yisrael, Hashem Elokeinu, Hashem
Echad![13] *[Hear, O Israel, the Lord is our God; the Lord is
One. This is the Jewish creed said when one faces mortal danger and on one's deathbed.] Everyone was certain
that this was the last minute of his life.*

Such a Shema Yisrael, *cried out from the depths of the
hearts of such varied people with such a wide range of
philosophies, I have never heard, and I ask God that this
recollection should be preserved in my memory forever.*

*During those wartime days, not only did everyone see
the workings of Divine Providence at every step, but one
could also see how the sound heart of a Jew is saturated
with genuine simple faith. Witnessing so manifestly how
powerfully and how profoundly a belief in God is rooted
in the heart of a Jew—that is the good that I learned
from the midst of the evil. The artless faith that sur-
faced in that universal outcry of* Shema Yisrael *opened
for me new wellsprings of love and reverence for the
Jewish sons and daughters, whoever they may be. My
deep conviction, based on factual proofs, is that the To-*

*rah-and-mitzvot heart of our fellow Jews is alive. It is
only that in some places they have grown faint, and the
task of rousing them is in the hands of inspiring speak-
ers, educators, and mentors.*[14]

Your outrage at tragedy indicates your underlying faith in God

You can identify your own recognition of God by the outrage you feel when a tragedy happens, whether to someone you know or to someone you don't know. Whether
you articulate the challenge out loud or simply think,
"Why do You allow this to happen?" you are acknowledging that God is calling the shots, and that you believe in
an all-powerful, just, and good[15] God Who controls the
affairs of human beings.

I'll go a step further. Even when you get upset about
an injustice done by one person to another, your sense of
outrage against the injustice acknowledges a God Who
sets the values of right and wrong. If there is no God, then
right and wrong comprise a mere convention, not an absolute. In fact, if God doesn't exist, no value is absolute. Life
is just one big crapshoot.

If you are a skeptic, you need to ask yourself an important question: Uncertain as I may be about God's existence,
what do I hope for in my heart of hearts that God *does*
exist or that God *doesn't* exist? If God exists, I am significant, and my actions are meaningful. If not, I am as a
fleeting speck of dust with no significance. This exercise
doesn't prove or disprove God's existence, but it does raise
a mirror in which you can look at yourself.

Finally, related to the question of free will, many people struggle to believe in God because He keeps Himself hidden. If God is real, they ask, why doesn't He show Himself?

Rabbi Aryeh Kaplan,* a brilliant and prolific writer on an enormous variety of Jewish topics, made the question of God's existence and behavior concrete in a very down-to-earth way in a short book he titled *If You Were God*. Kaplan presented a simple, clear understanding of how God's predilection for keeping Himself hidden is connected to man's freedom of choice:

> *If God were to reveal Himself, then man would no longer be able to exist as a free entity.*
>
> *As long as He is hidden, we can strive toward Him and attain the Godly. But we do this as a matter of free choice, and we are not overwhelmed by it. But if God were to reveal Himself, then man would no longer be able to exist as a free entity. He would know that he was always under the scrutiny of his Master, and that would make him into something less than human. He would become some kind of puppet or robot, with an essential ingredient of his humanness destroyed.*
>
> *Many people say that they would believe if only they could witness some sign or miracle. Sinai showed us that even this is not enough if people do not want to believe.*

---

* **Rabbi Aryeh Kaplan, 1934–1983:** American rabbi, author, and physicist. Rabbi Kaplan authored more than fifty volumes on Torah, Talmud, Jewish mysticism, and philosophy, many of which have become modern-day classics. He is best known for his popular translation and elucidation of the Bible, *The Living Torah*, and his translation of the Ladino biblical commentary, *Me'am Lo'ez*.

*From all this we can begin to understand one of the
most basic restrictions that God imposes upon Himself.
He is a hidden God and does not reveal Himself. This
is required by man's psychology as well as God's very
purpose in creation. God reveals Himself only to such
people whose faith is so great that the revelation will
make no difference to their belief.*

In other words, if God were visible, there would be no
freedom of choice. We would all be like Pavlov's dogs, sal-
ivating on cue. God's challenge is to be hidden enough so
that His presence doesn't overwhelm us, but it is—if we
choose it—a conscious, driving force in the world and in
our lives. It's the difference between staring directly into
the noon sun and looking at a sunset. The former can burn
your retinas, but the latter filters the sun enough so that
you can experience it as beautiful, not threatening.

God also wants to keep people on their best behavior. If
you're smart, you don't drive eighty miles per hour next to
a police car. That's easy advice to follow if the police are in
a black-and-white, but God drives in an unmarked vehicle. If you don't think there's a police car near you and you
choose to go eighty miles per hour, you might get away
with it. On the other hand, you will soon realize you are
not getting away with it when the officer in the unmarked
car turns on the flashing lights and gives chase.

**The believer only has to explain the existence of
God. The atheist has to explain everything else.**

God doesn't want to be visible or easily provable, but God
does want to be understood. King David instructs his son

Solomon, *Know the God of your father and serve Him with a complete heart and an eager soul, for God examines all hearts and understands the thoughts of every creation. If you seek Him, He will be found by you.*[16] God wants an intimate relationship with each of us. That starts with being understood. For this reason, He acts as a father who wants a relationship with his young child. To do that, God must come down, so to speak, to engage at the child's level. And yet, He must be the one in charge.

It's only natural that in our irreverent, scientific age, belief in God suggests falling for something fundamentally irrational. That fear poses a seemingly insurmountable obstacle to belief in God for many people.

To a degree, they are correct. As we pointed out at the beginning of this chapter, there is no absolute proof that there is a God. That's why coming to believe in God is called a "leap of faith," not a "crawl of faith!" But it is not irrational to believe that there is a God. In fact, belief in God is completely consistent with logical thought. Logic concedes that reason has its limits, and when it is applied to God, Who created logic and reason, reason itself is insufficient to encompass Him. Therefore, an intelligent, rational person does not have to give up his or her rational, critical thinking in order to believe in God. Therefore, while no one can prove God's existence, neither can anyone disprove it. Lack of empirical proof doesn't mean there is no God. A rational case can be made that God's existence defies proof. Don't forget, too, that atheism itself is a *belief* that there is no God. That can't be proven either.

In a conversation with a student of Rabbi Nota Schiller—one of the founders of Ohr Somayach, a *yeshivah* in Jerusalem for non-observant Jews who are studying Torah and religious practice, often for the first time, the student shared with me how Rabbi Schiller summed up the case for belief succinctly: "I'm ninety percent intellectually convinced of the existence of God and the Divine origin of the Torah, and my momentum takes me the rest of the way."

The arguments both for and against the existence of God have been around for thousands of years and will continue until Mashiach—the Messiah—arrives. There's an expression I really relate to: "The believer only has to explain the existence of God. The atheist has to explain the existence of everything else."

God and misfortune can and do coexist. The presence of one does not preclude the presence of the other. Believing in God isn't a "Get out of jail free" card, nor is it a guarantor that nothing bad will ever happen to a person. We Jews believe in a God Who is One—Who is responsible for *everything* in the world, including good *and* evil. We may not—we cannot—understand God fully. This idea seems to be widely shared. Even the great Southern singer and songwriter Garth Brooks has written, "Just because He may not answer doesn't mean He don't care." The triple negative and grammatical issues aside, He exists, He cares, and He is beyond our ability to completely understand.

Chapter Summary: *People struggle with belief in God for many reasons, including a lack of religious education beyond that which was given in childhood, or an intellectual resistance to the idea of an all-powerful, good God Who allows tragedy and evil. No one can prove the existence of God, although it's arguably easier to offer evidence for a Creator than to prove atheism. God also needs to remain hidden, so to speak, so that we can maintain our free will.*

~~

Endnotes:

1   Daniel 7:9.

2   Robert Jastrow, *God and the Astronomers*, new and expanded edition (New York, NY: Norton, 2000).

3   Unpublished transcript of a speech by Rabbi Adin Even-Israel Steinsaltz, Brussels, April 1985; translated to English from the original Hebrew. Transcript provided by the Steinsaltz Center, Jerusalem.

4   From *This Is My God* by Herman Wouk, copyright © 1987. Reprinted by permission of Little, Brown and Company, an imprint of Hachette Book Group, Inc.

5   Deuteronomy 5:4.

6   Deuteronomy 5:3.

7   Exodus 19:9.

8   *Mishneh Torah*, Laws of the Fundamentals of the Torah 8:1.

9   Numbers 14:22; *Avot* 5:4.

10   Genesis 50:19–20.

11   Psalms 94:8–10.

12   *Rosh Hashanah* 16b.

13   Deuteronomy 6:4.

14   *Sefer Hasichot Kayitz* 5700 (1940) (Brooklyn, NY: Kehot Publication Society, 1947).

15   See Exodus 34:6; Jonah 4:2.

16   I Chronicles 28:9.

CHAPTER FIVE

Is It Okay to Be Angry with God?

My God, my God, why have You forsaken me? Why
are You so far from helping me? Why are You so
far from the words of my cry? My God! I call out by
day, but You answer not; and at night, but there is
no respite for me.
                                        —*Psalms 22:2–3*

In 1969, psychiatrist Elisabeth Kübler-Ross identified five
stages of grief[1]—denial, anger, bargaining, depression, and
acceptance—which have become a familiar guide to the
mourning process. Denial is the spontaneous response to
tragedy. We refuse to accept that something terrible has
happened to us. How can I wake up in the morning and
find that my child is gone? How can illness take both my
parents within weeks? How could the life of a young person with such a brilliant future be ended in the blink of
an eye? These are rhetorical questions that are asked in a
state of shock and disbelief. Denial is a protective mecha-
nism that prevents the magnitude of the tragedy from hitting us all at once. Disbelief filters the pain and provides
a momentary respite before the full burden of reality sets
in.

Once we can no longer pretend that it didn't happen,
and after the tragedy hits home, we move to the stage of
anger.

Identify your anger and learn to release it in a healthy and productive way

In this chapter, we will take a look at that anger, to whom it is directed, and how it can actually be positive as we struggle to get through the hard times. Anger can be directed inward, where the hurt and suffering build up and it seems there is no way to let it out. This inward-directed anger is like the contents of a pressure cooker, boiling and churning as the pressure rises dangerously, while the outside *appears* calm. Of course, it is not only counterproductive but destructive to live with such turmoil. It can lead to a host of mental and emotional issues, often including depression and damaged relationships, to list but a few.

Another approach to the anger is to direct it outward as we cry out—and look for someone to blame. Often, that "someone" is God, Whom we identify as the source of this injustice. After all, He is in charge, isn't He? Is there another manager above Him to whom we can register a complaint? It's easy to see how a person can embrace this outward-directed anger in the face of such deep pain. We might even rant and rave at the God Whom we revere and worship and pray to—the God Who seems to have abandoned us.

Since anger is so visceral and such a common and understandable reaction, it's important that we identify it and then channel it purposefully, to let it play out in a healthy and productive way. This will also help to prevent that anger from bursting out dangerously, possibly injuring those closest to us.

Sometimes we refuse to recognize the anger at all. We

may have trouble acknowledging our feelings, since we don't want to admit to ourselves that we are angry at God, the same God Whom we want to get to know and love.

Rabbi Zev Schostak, director of pastoral care at the Gurwin Jewish Nursing and Rehabilitation Center in Commack, New York, wrote the following powerful story in *Jewish Action*,[2] the Orthodox Union's magazine:

> Sam Gordon was a truly devout eighty-six-year-old man who rarely missed a religious service and who performed mitzvot (commandments) with enthusiasm, despite his poor health. Sam was a long-term resident in our nursing home who suffered from serious cardiac and respiratory illnesses. Yet, against often insurmountable odds, his strong faith prevailed, and he observed mitzvot without fail.
>
> Not long after Sam's eighty-seventh birthday, there was a dramatic decline in his respiratory condition. It became clear that he would have to spend the rest of his life on a mechanical ventilator. For Sam, whose faith was his raison d'être, this devastating development meant that he would be tethered to a machine on the vent unit and would never again be able to regularly attend religious services.
>
> When I visited Sam, he was downcast and meditative—a far cry from the ebullient and outgoing senior whom we had all come to know.
>
> "Rabbi, I'm so glad you stopped by. I really wanted to speak with you. Did you hear the bad news?" Sam asked. (I had already heard that Sam was being placed on a ventilator, but it was important for me to know how Sam had taken it. I wanted to have him tell me the news in his own words.)

"No, Sam, what bad news?"

"Rabbi, my breathing is worse, and my pulmonologist told me that the only way I can continue to live is if I'm attached to a ventilator, which will help my lungs work. Without it, I'm dead! But with it, I might as well be dead! I'm going to be stuck in my room on this unit forever. I won't be able to attend daily services and your holiday programs. I'll never be able to take leave and join my family for an occasional holiday!" Sam raised his voice. "Is that right, Rabbi? Is this just?"

"You sound angry. Are you angry, Sam?"

"At whom?"

I paused briefly. "At God."

"God ... How can I be angry at God? I'm a religious man. God must know what He's doing, that's what I believe. So how can I be angry with Him?"

"I'm asking you again, Sam—are you angry?"

Sam didn't answer, because he knew that I knew what he must have been thinking. The expression on his face and the tone of his voice said it all.

"Sam, you're angry. You're angry with God for doing this to you, but you're afraid to admit it."

I waited for him to respond. He was stone-faced.

"You're a religious man. Let me ask you a question: Do you believe that God knows what's on your mind and what you're feeling?" He nodded in the affirmative.

"In that case, God knows you're angry with Him even if you don't say a word. Right? But that's okay, Sam, because God knows why you're angry with Him, and He

understands." Sam nodded again, listening closely to my
words but still unwilling to admit to his anger.

"Sam, it's okay to tell God that you're upset with Him.
Remember, you're not telling Him something that He
doesn't know anyway! But just keep speaking to Him.
Keep the lines of communication open. Don't worry
about God becoming angry with you when He hears
your complaints. He can take it. He's got big shoulders!"

It was sink-or-swim time, and I couldn't afford to sink

Like Sam, I also had difficulty facing my own feelings
when my thirty-six-year-old wife passed away. I saw myself as strong and stoic, and as a lifelong believing Jew. I
was even a rabbi and director of a religious school! Yet I
resisted allowing myself to be angry at God. Rather, I was
in deep shock and pain, bewildered by the new and in-
tensely challenging circumstances suddenly thrust upon
me and my family. I didn't have the emotional language to
articulate my feelings at that time. But as I imagine you
have experienced, when you don't express important, urgent feelings, they eat away at you. The more you push
them away, the more damage they can cause, psychologically and physically.

I was dejected. But it was not a static sadness. It al-
ternated between a feeling of turmoil (*"Why is this happening?"*), and a gloominess tied to grief. Yet I was not
the type of person who could pull the blanket over my
head and say, "I'm not getting out of bed today." I had
eleven children depending on me. I also headed a school

with almost four hundred students. It was sink-or-swim time, and I couldn't afford to sink—that would have taken the ship down with me. My children, the students at the school, the rest of the staff, and the parents weren't about to accept that "Rabbi Schusterman is sad today, so he can't deal with your problems. You'll just have to take a number and wait your turn until he's feeling ready." So rather than sink, I swam. I could not let the inevitable chaos take hold. I put my feelings on hold, visiting them only periodically when it felt safe to do so.

Only later did I realize that the malaise I was experiencing was disappointment with God, which led to my distancing and alienation from Him. In a way, I felt betrayed by God, and upon reflection I think I was giving Him the cold shoulder. My mind had answers to all my unarticulated questions—as a rabbi I knew all the basic answers. But my heart was suffering its own very personal pain. My emotions had a path of their own, and this path wasn't quite as generous and accepting as my intellectually focused, rabbinical brain. I could still appreciate God's ultimate goodness as an article of faith, but that appreciation was more cerebral than emotional. My heart could not engage in the same way.

Those first months after Rochel Leah's death were the hardest months of my life. They were made more difficult by the fact that I was almost always surrounded by people. The only times that I was really alone were before I went to bed, by which time, having dealt with my students and their parents, teachers, and my eleven children, I was too exhausted to think. I was also alone in my car during the fifteen-minute drive from home to the Hebrew Academy.

One morning while driving on the freeway to my school—don't tell this to the Highway Patrol—I was reading a belated condolence card from my wife's brother and his wife, whose poignant authenticity touched me so deeply that I burst out crying. I had to pull over and stop the car for a few minutes to regain my composure. The card read:

It's okay to be afraid
    of things you don't understand.

It's okay to feel anxious
    when things aren't working your way.

It's okay to feel lonely ...
    even when you're with people.

It's okay to feel unfulfilled
    because you know something is missing
    (even when you're not sure what it is).

It's okay to think and worry and cry.

It's okay to do
    whatever you have to do, but

just remember, too ...
    that eventually you're going to
    adjust to the changes life brings your way.

And you'll realize that
    it's okay to love again and laugh again,

and it's okay to get to the point where
    the life you live
    is full and satisfying and good to you ...

> *and it will be that way*
>> *because you made it that way.*

So many of these pithy phrases articulated my feelings that I couldn't put words to. Viewed from the rut I was in, the optimistic, hopeful vision seemed like an unattainable dream.

It was then that I realized that I couldn't do this by myself. I felt like a person who had half of himself amputated and was unable to regain his balance. I needed reassurance that what I was feeling was "normal," whatever that meant.

I sought out a therapist who fit my requirements. I needed someone I could relate to. I wanted to speak to someone who had, like me, lost a spouse and was raising children alone. I found such a person. Though she had retired, mutual acquaintances convinced her to take me on. For the next six months, every two weeks, I drove an hour each way to West Los Angeles for an hour-long session.

"How are you ... *really*?"

As time passed, I thought I had things under control, but about four years after Rochel Leah's passing, I found out otherwise. I had by then remarried to Chana Rachel, a wonderful and wise woman.

I had been introduced to Chana Rachel Baron by my sister Nechoma Greisman, who lived in Jerusalem. Originally a New Yorker from Washington Heights, Chana Rachel had lived in Jerusalem for eight years and was teaching in a women's seminary. She also knew my sister well. Almost a year after Rochel Leah's passing, Nechoma visited me in California to see how I was doing.

We talked about many things during the few days she was with me, including my thoughts on remarriage. Little did I know that my very caring sister had an agenda, and Chana Rachel *was* the agenda. Chana Rachel was single and wanted to get married, but only to the right person, whom she hadn't yet met. My sister's name, Nechoma, means "consolation" in Hebrew, and she lived up to her name once again in this situation. She knew both of us well and saw the possibility of our marrying as a probability. When Nechoma returned home, she explored with Chana Rachel the possibility that I might be her Mr. Right. And so it was.

Before we married, a close friend asked me about her. "Who in her right mind would uproot herself from Jerusalem to marry a guy with eleven children to raise in Southern California?"

I said, "She'd have to be insane or an angel, and crazy she isn't." Being single and not having had children, she courageously dove into the challenge of helping to raise a large family.

Kind and wise though Chana Rachel was, my obligations of running a school with hundreds of students and trying to deal with my own many children meant that she carried the lion's share of the work. She was suddenly the mother of many children, each of whom carried their own trauma, and doing a remarkable job of nurturing her new, huge family. Yet it certainly came at a cost. My obligations at work and home meant I had been shortchanging Chana

Rachel of "together-alone time," when newlyweds usually bond in their first years of marriage. We decided that
while the children were in summer camp, we would take
a two-week trip to Israel, together-alone, to remedy that.

We were strolling along in Rothschild Square, a relatively quiet, off-the-beaten-track area in the Old City of
Jerusalem, when my wife looked at me and asked, "How
are you?"

"*Baruch Hashem,* thank God, I'm fine," I replied.

Chana Rachel paused, looked into my eyes knowingly,
and repeated, "How are you ... *really*?"

That *really* pierced my shell. I paused to reflect before
replying, and suddenly I felt weak and dizzy. The color
drained from my face, and the whole world seemed to be
spinning around me. At that moment, I reexperienced the
entire course of events of the previous four years as they
flashed before me. I was able to look inside myself, which
is when I realized that I still held a lot of hurt that had
built up a lot of deep emotional pressure. Although physically I was a half a world away from my daily stresses,
I was having an emotional breakdown—brief, but very
real. I realized that the six months of therapy I had gone
through had been a good start, but it wasn't enough. I
needed someone else to talk to and with whom I could
work things out.

We cannot suppress our pain forever; it needs to be released

I tracked down a therapist whom I had known casually
in Los Angeles. She had made *aliyah*—immigrated to Is-

rael—and now had a private practice in Jerusalem. Over the next ten days I visited her five times, two hours each time. She asked wise questions and I answered, the words pouring out from my heart. Her prompting questions helped me to relieve myself of deep, pent-up emotions, enabling me to talk out my hurt and somehow sort out my issues. Those were intense sessions, but she was a skilled facilitator safely guiding me toward unloading the pain that I had been carrying around for years. I realized that I had been suppressing the burden of my disappointment with where life's detour had taken me and my disappointment with God, which led to my self-imposed distancing from Him. It was a heavy price to pay.

In those sessions I learned that I could release God, as it were, from the grudge I was holding against Him. Even with these painful feelings, I realized that I needed God. I recognized that I no longer had the need for Him to apologize or explain Himself to me. For my own sake, I realized that I also needed to release myself from my grudge and renew our relationship unfettered. These realizations allowed me to return gradually to my balanced self.

This type of evaluation happens in human relationships, too. When we are offended by a close friend, a parent, or a spouse, and a sincere apology is not forthcoming, we calculate internally the value of the relationship versus the burden of the offense. Some friendships end this way. In others, we decide that the value of the relationship far outweighs the perceived offense. We choose to release that burden or grudge and resume the relationship.

I realize that my "fast-tracked" therapy is not the usual way. It can take many weeks, months, or sometimes years to fully unpack the emotional pain and baggage that has worn you down. I was extremely fortunate that I had gone through six months of previous counseling, which I believe made it possible for this intense, short period of therapy to work for me.

This is how I worked through what Kübler-Ross called the depression phase. There are two kinds of depression. One is the episodic type that comes and goes, as mine did, but still allows us to get out of bed and do what we are expected to do on any given day. That's what I believe I went through. Then there is the other, darker form of clinical depression, in which we are unable to perform our activities of daily living. Whatever form your depression might take, it's crucial to get counseling. Talking these things through with a trained professional, a member of the clergy, or a caring wise person helps us unburden ourselves of an unbearable emotional load and process our pain and other unresolved feelings. Depression seldom lifts on its own without doing lasting damage. People need to reach out and get help.

Would it have been better if I had railed at God early on, expressing my frustration and sadness? Should I have confronted a God Whose plan took my wife away too soon and so suddenly? Would it have been better for me if I had told God how I felt instead of letting the feelings fester inside me? Perhaps. But my self-image wouldn't allow me to become the kind of person who could be angry with God, and I never wanted God to think I was angry with Him. But as I learned, sometimes we *must* express our emotions to protect our sanity and health. These feelings have an impact on our relationships, whether the relationship is with another human being, with God, or with ourselves. Therefore, we must engage in this process with honesty.

Consider the following incident:

Jack had been married to his wife Judy for seven years. It appeared to Judy that in recent months Jack had become less and less attentive to her. At a party, Jack was curt with Judy in front of other people, which she found humiliating. She had suspicions, albeit unfounded, that he was seeing someone else. She had thought they had a good marriage, but his recent coolness was disconcerting. Judy scrutinized her own behavior to see if she had in some way contributed to the rough patch in their relationship, but after honest introspection, she truly could not see any change in her attitude or behavior that would have contributed to Jack's straying.

She told her husband that they had to go to counseling, and he agreed.

As they sat down facing the counselor and after going through the preliminaries, Judy took the lead and said:

> *I quite understand Jack's behavior; it's my fault. It has been quite a while since I made a special candlelight dinner just for the two of us. Perhaps I put on a few pounds in the last year or two and have not been maintaining my figure as I should. I may have neglected him when he was going through difficulties at work. Is it a surprise that Jack feels hurt? I will change my ways so that we can put our marriage back on track.*

But it was all a sham; she didn't mean a word she said!

Judy's truth was that she felt deeply hurt. She wanted to pound on Jack's chest and yell:

Jack, I love you, I want you, and I need you. How can you do this to me? How can you do this to us? We are one. You committed to me for life, as I did to you. I won't give you up nor will I let you off easily.

I don't know all of what is going on inside of you. If it's something in me, tell me. I know I'm not perfect, but I don't think there's been any neglect on my part. If there's anything I can do to facilitate you getting back on track, tell me. If you have to do it on your own, do it. Do whatever it takes, as long as the result will be that we will truly be together again, like when we were young, starry-eyed dreamers and lovers.

Sometimes we have a rough patch in our relationship with God

If Judy knew deep down that Jack was hers for life, this second speech is the one she would have given. She would have felt confident that she could get through to him and end up in his loving embrace with a new beginning. She would have had the confidence to remind him of the strength of their bond and its deep foundation. She would have let go of her anger, which would have helped her strengthen their union.

But Judy was insecure with their relationship, uncertain about what Jack felt deep inside of him, so she was afraid to press the issue lest she hasten the end of their marriage. She tried to take refuge by creating a false set of problems, things she could fix herself. That might have calmed things in the short time, but it would have guaranteed a lack of true intimacy in the long term.

I tell this story because I think it is a good analogy to our relationship with God (although this dynamic occurs in marriages all too often). We must have the confidence in our commitment to God and His commitment to us to forge a strong and meaningful relationship.

It may feel counterintuitive, but our ability to cry out to God is actually proof of the strength of our relationship. Think about it: If we were not so invested in the relationship, we wouldn't feel free to cry, in either bitterness or pain. But *because* we believe in Him, *because* we are convinced that He believes in us also, and *because* we believe there is right and wrong and that right must triumph, we *can* shout, or cry, or start an "argument," so to speak. Even during times when we need to express blame and negative feelings, we must say what we mean. The important thing is that we know we can rely on our mutual commitment and the strength of our relationship with God to get us through this rough patch.

What happens if you are a moral and just person and you perceive injustice? You have two options. The first option: You have to speak out, regardless of what the issue is. You can't worry about how others might react. A just person is compelled to speak out against injustice because injustice cannot stand. It's wrong!

The second option: Ignore it. But another way of saying "ignore it" is "repress it." Don't deal with it. Tamp it down to where you can't get at it. When you repress something, one of two things happens. If it's small, it gets absorbed, relegated to the garbage heap of repressed issues buried within each of us. But if the problem is big, it will burst out later, on a day when you have not scheduled a major outburst on your calendar. On that day that you cannot predict, many repressed feelings will explode. This is an expression of the repressed depression, which is anger turned inward. One way or another, it will come out.

A case in point: At the Hebrew Academy where I was director, a parent lost his father, an elderly Holocaust survivor, quite unexpectedly. "David" flew from Southern California to Montreal for the funeral on a Thursday and returned to his family before Shabbat the next day. That year, the two-day festival of Shavuot happened to begin immediately after Shabbat, which meant that the normal seven-day *shivah* mourning period was truncated to only Friday. One does not sit *shivah* on Shabbat or Shavuot, nor does *shivah* pick up again after the festival. This meant that David went back to his usual activities having only sat *shivah* for a few hours.

I saw him during the week he returned and asked him how he was doing. At first glance, he seemed fine. But a few weeks later, his wife called and told me that he had suffered a nervous breakdown and was hospitalized in a psychiatric ward for severe depression. When I visited him, he shared with me that his depression was related to the unfinished business he had with his father, with whom he hadn't spoken for several weeks before his death. Because he didn't sit *shivah* for the entire week but only for a much-abbreviated time, he hadn't had enough time to process his father's passing and work through his feelings about it. That weighed him down until he collapsed.

This helps explain the traditional phrase of consolation that Jews say to mourners, which begins *HaMakom yenachem es'chem,* meaning, "May the Almighty console you." Here, God is referred to as *HaMakom,* the "Place" or the "Space," because God is everywhere—He fills every place and all space.

Why do we use this metaphor of "Place" or "Space" for God rather than *Ado-noi,* "my Lord," or *Hashem,* "the Name," as God is usually referred to? I heard one reason that is attributed to the Lubavitcher Rebbe, Rabbi Menachem Mendel Schneerson, who explained when paying a *shivah* visit: *HaMakom* refers to God the Omnipresent, Who fills all space and place. The mourner experiences a void—a lonely, empty space in his soul, in his core. We say to the mourner that, ultimately, only *HaMakom,* the omnipresent God, can fill the void in a grieving person's being. This is not only a kind wish but also advice to the mourner. If you can realize and absorb the idea that God hasn't abandoned you to your grief but is actually with you in your void, in your pain and loneliness, then you can find great support in your suffering. You can begin to fill the void in your heart.

Even a full week of *shivah* would probably not have been enough time for David to resolve the unsettled issues he had with his father. But he would have had much more time to process the loss. Friends in his community would have sat with him to offer comfort. He could have shared stories about his father, even those that might have offered some catharsis. And he would have had the comfort of *HaMakom*, Who is there to lean on at all times. His emotional healing would have had a stronger, healthier start.

This is why Judaism places such importance on the *shivah* period. We recognize how crucial it is to begin to process the loss and to benefit from the presence of consolers, as well as *the* Consoler—God. This time gives us the space we require to begin this work, without the distractions of our careers, a sudden immersion into a festival, or other elements of "normal" life.

Even Abraham and Moses each had a "crisis of faith"

The painful loss of a loved one can sometimes lead to a crisis of faith. What does Judaism teach us about dealing with these circumstances? We find the Jewish answer when we recall what Abraham did and what Moses did when they each went through what we might call in modern terminology a "crisis of faith."

Each of them boldly spoke up and said, "God, I don't know why You're doing this. By the very values You teach us, what You did is obviously wrong, and I'm challenging You. How is it that the Judge, the Just Creator of the world, shall do injustice?"[3] This was how Abraham argued with God when He announced that He would destroy Sodom because nearly all of its inhabitants were cruel and evil. This was how Moses protested when God threatened to destroy the Israelites after they made and worshipped the Golden Calf—a symbol of idol worship. Moses demanded, "Forgive them! And if not, please erase me from Your book—the Torah—that You have written!"

Both Abraham and Moses understood that God *wanted* them to argue with Him.

Not only is arguing with God a healthy and normal response to such extreme circumstances, but it also reflects the best of Jewish traditions. These responses demonstrate the intimacy in the relationship between a Jew and God. Abraham, the first of the Jewish patriarchs; Moses, our first leader; King David, the author of Psalms; and especially Job, whose name has become synonymous with suffering. Each one challenges God's behavior when they perceive that He allows unwarranted suffering. Even Tevye, the dairyman of Sholem Aleichem's story upon which the musical *Fiddler on the Roof* was based, was portrayed as a simple, unschooled Jew. Yet Tevye criticizes God with the intimacy reserved only for a very dear friend.

Of course, it is easier to challenge God in the midst of an unfolding crisis than it is to cry out to God after a tragedy has already occurred. In the midst of something bad unfolding, you can stand up and shout, "Stop, God! The lesson You are trying to teach me is not working!" Or even, "Stop, God! What You are doing is wrong!" But when you're reeling from a disaster that has already occurred, you have to figure out how to deal with it, how to submit to it, as did Job: *God has given and God has taken; may God's name be blessed.*[4] In the very next verse—*Despite all this, Job did not sin nor ascribe impropriety to God*[5]—we see that Job offered no reproach to God. When you are speaking after the fact, you have fewer choices how to respond, fewer opportunities to ask for a different outcome.

God is the ultimate Counselor—here to listen

We have probably all been guilty at one time or another of being grumpy, miserable, or even lashing out in anger over trivial mishaps. After a restless and frustrating night's sleep, when the toast burns, the hot coffee spills, the tire is flat, the boss is mad, and just about everything seems to be going wrong, we might take it out on people we love just because they happen to be in the room. Is that healthy anger? In a limited way, but *only* because we get it out of our system quickly, and our fragile equilibrium is restored. But later, we must apologize to our blameless victims! Other than the benefit of catharsis, this kind of anger is inappropriate, immature, and unhealthy. It is equally as immature and inappropriate to throw a tantrum before God over something trivial.

Happily, God is like a wise and patient parent and gives each of us a pass, recognizing our built-in inadequacies. We need to save confrontations with God exclusively for the messy, big, seemingly unmanageable problems and traumas in our lives. We need to keep perspective on what is a real "problem" versus what is just a passing inconvenience.

When God is real to me, I know that He won't disintegrate when I'm miserable and express my misery informally, lacking appropriate decorum. When I am confident in my relationship with God, then complaining to Him or blaming Him for what happened to me won't harm either of us. God won't abandon a mortal soul over a few words of anger or blame. God can take the hit. The Almighty will remain the all-knowing, all-powerful God He is. As they say in the fellowship of Alcoholics Anonymous, another place where individuals must confront their relationship with a Higher Power, "If your God can't handle your anger, get yourself a bigger God!"

Our venting will make us feel better as we yell and cry and point fingers in blame. God, in His infinite wisdom, will simply listen. He will not be offended, because He knows our emotions. *We* are the ones who are afraid, shocked at the words of malice that sprang from our mouths when we let it all out. We fear that we will be turning our backs on God—Whom we love—by lashing out. But in reality, our angry accusations, tears, and yelling are the first cathartic steps that will allow us to process the grief we are feeling.

God is the Counselor; He is here to listen.

The Book of Psalms is full of such anguished cries, like this one:

Awaken! Why should You sleep, O Lord?

Arouse Yourself, forsake not forever.

Why do You hide Your face, forgetting our affliction and oppression?

For our soul is cast down to the dust; our belly clings to the earth.

Arise to assist us and redeem us for the sake of Your kindness.[6]

King David wrote most of the one hundred fifty Psalms

and was the book's editor. The Psalms are full of emotion, sometimes fear, rage, and sorrow. They usually end with hope and optimism. No one was a more appropriate choice for writing and editing them than King David. In these poetic, heartfelt pieces, he was speaking on his own behalf about his very difficult life. He was also speaking prophetically about the future Jewish people. Jews have turned to the Psalms throughout their turbulent history to frame their thoughts and feelings in prayer.

The Psalms not only ask God to resolve the challenges that King David faces—and, by extension, those that the Jews face; the Psalms also pose forceful challenges to God, confronting Him when He seems not to respond to the needy supplicant. For example:

> *A psalm by David: My God, my God, why have You forsaken me?*
>
> *Why are You so far from saving me?*
>
> *In You our fathers trusted, and You delivered them.*
>
> *But You, God, be not far.*
>
> *O my Strength, hasten to my assistance!*[7]

Many of the Psalms are open-ended; not all conclude with certainty that the prayers would be answered or with upbeat sentiments or expressions of absolute faith. Yet King David was not afraid to write them, and suffering people throughout the millennia have been touched by their resonant, deep emotion. Even today, in times of need, Jews recite the Psalms in tears, asking along with the Psalmist, "Why are you neglecting me?" All the while, they sense that God is listening to their prayers even as they aren't being answered.

These questions and petitions to God are part of the Jewish canon, cherished aspects of our relationship with Him. They are not rejected as blasphemy. We do not curse God because we feel like we no longer love Him. We curse the evil that He allows to happen. Challenging God during a time of need shows the strength in our belief and trust in Him, not weakness. It shows that during our lowest moments we still—especially then—turn to Him. Even though what we say might be unkind, we are crying on the biggest shoulders in the world, refusing to give up on this most critical relationship. God understands that what we are really asking is for Him to help us get through the dark times, to hold our hands as we travel untested, rocky emotional terrain and to escort us safely through to the other side.

The soul abhors a vacuum

Most people *need* to go through this process, to put their minds at rest before they are able to move on. But there are also some people who don't want to look deeper. They just say, "Well, stuff happens." "The tragedy was simply bad luck." "There's no one—no One—to blame." I believe that people who limit their thinking about gaping, painful losses to such statements haven't filled the holes in their souls. They move on but forget that the human psyche and soul abhor a vacuum. Eventually, that hole will be like a black hole in the universe, its gravitational pull sucking up everything—even light—within range. We urgently need the light of insight and enlightenment, the peace and tranquility of being held in God's embrace. This is what will ultimately lead a person out of the darkness of despair to the light of hope.

Let's look at the analogy of a person who has unresolved issues after a tragedy and compare him to a car. The emptied space in his soul can knock his chassis out of alignment and cause an accident the next time he hits an emotional pothole. He might fill the hole with alcohol or drugs, gumming up the engine. Without knowing it, he might hold on to anger issues, clogging the filters that allow the car to run smoothly. This person needs a team of good "mechanics": clergy to discuss spiritual matters with, such as his relationship with God; a psychotherapist for insight into his emotional reactions; and supportive friends to help fill some of the emptiness caused by the loss of a relationship.

The Talmud teaches, "He who gets angry is as if he worships idols."[8] This sounds extreme, doesn't it? After all, we have spent most of this chapter acknowledging the value and importance of expressing disappointment and even anger—including at God—for the pain and difficulties in our lives, as well as for evil and injustice in the world around us. But the anger the Talmud criticizes is that of a person who believes that the forces in the world exist and function independently of God. Acknowledging the supposed power of these outside forces is the very definition of idolatry.

Getting angry at the circumstances alone, as if they happened by themselves rather than coming from God, denies that there is a purpose and a lesson inherent in everything. We are meant to learn from all our circumstances. Most people, when looking at their lives in retrospect, will acknowledge that they have learned and grown more from their difficult and painful experiences than from their pleasant and happy ones.

Excuse me, God, but Your justice doesn't seem to be working right now ...

As a Jew, I may appeal to God respectfully and humbly when I see injustice that clashes with the values that God Himself has set forth in the Torah. But in doing so, I am not trying to separate from God—as I might be if I were angry with another person and possibly basking in my self-righteous indignation. In my challenge, I am seeking true unity with God, appealing to Him to live up to the standards that He established and taught. I am saying, "I'm with You all the way in Your justice, but why isn't it working—or why doesn't it seem to be working—in this instance?" If my question is sincere and my purpose is to be more like Him, then God will cut me some slack even if I use a challenging tone.

Abraham, Moses, and Job did not get clear responses or resolutions to their challenges, but they remained as faithful to God as they were before. How were they able to do this? Was God ignoring them?

No, He was not, but this question brings us back to Dr. Kübler-Ross' stages, the fifth and ultimate one being acceptance. Psychologically and religiously, we must eventually accept God's mastery over everything, including life and death and the circumstances by which God's ways occur. Naturally, it is much harder and takes longer to reach acceptance after a tragedy, but working to achieve this stage is essential to restore calmness in the soul.

Unless the angry person engages in significant introspection and reflection, the anger that accompanies tragedy will remain rooted to the soul. In my view, this introspection and reflection on one's purpose and meaning in life is the only effective antidote to the rising bile that breeds and feeds the anger.

Not convinced? Just look at the people in your life who hold grudges, who are nursing an old emotional injury for all it's worth. They can keep the raw anger aflame for years, even decades! But you see that their anger is corrosive to them—body, psyche, and soul. It corrodes their relationships. Work to move beyond the anger for your own sake. Letting go of anger, no matter how justified it may have been originally, removes a barrier to having a relationship with God.

Anger stemming from tragedy or misfortune cannot be ignored or suppressed. When we let go by expressing it from a place of belief and commitment to God, this is a healthy response. The key is not to get stuck in the anger, unable to move to the next phase of processing grief that comes right afterward: negotiation (*"God, if only You could undo this tragedy, I'll be a better person"*), and, ultimately, acceptance.

Acceptance does not mean that we are happy about what happened, but we can arrive at a point where we can acknowledge the *reality* of what has happened. Ultimately, we may even come to recognize and accept God's role in the occurrence of that event. This way, we can continue to live our lives again and focus on something other than the great pain over our loss that never seems to lift.

Sometimes you hear people speak of "closure." I don't believe that true closure exists, if that term means that you feel the loss is truly one hundred percent behind you and you never think about it anymore. Losses almost always come back to cause pain. Like waves at the ocean's shore, they seem to get smaller and smaller, but then suddenly another huge wave occurs. Don't get disheartened if the recurrence of the *yahrtzeit*—the anniversary of the date of death—triggers the old feelings. Certainly, festivals, anniversaries, and other special dates can do the same. Feelings of pain, loss, and, yes, even anger suddenly surge for no particular reason. This is normal.

If you feel that you are still using a teaspoon to drain an ocean of anger, I am here to reassure you that eventually you will gain a foothold on your life again without being utterly consumed by the anger and the pain. If your loss is recent, though, that moment may feel as if it is a long way off.

But it will come. I assure you; it will come.

Chapter Summary: *Anger is a natural phase in the grieving process, and it may last a long time before it is resolved. That anger can also be directed toward God. Though anger is, ultimately, self-destructive, it's necessary to work through this stage of grief until you reach a stage of acceptance of the circumstances. Being angry with God doesn't threaten the relationship with Him. As with any other close and primary relationship, expressing anger* *or disbelief can be cathartic and healing, and it can reflect the level of closeness between you and the Other.*

Endnotes:

1   Elisabeth Kübler-Ross, *On Death and Dying: What the Dying Have to Teach Doctors, Nurses, Clergy, and Their Own Families* (1st edition – New York, NY: Charles Scribner's Sons Publishing, 1969).

2   Rabbi Zev Schostak, "Holding On or Letting Go: Reflections on Hospice in the Jewish Tradition," *Jewish Action*, Vol. 69, no. 3 (Spring 5769/2009).

3   This quote is a paraphrase. The final sentence is more directly from the Torah, from Genesis 18:25.

4   Job 1:21.

5   Ibid. 1:22.

6   Psalms 44:24–27.

7   Psalms 22:1, 2, 5, 20.

8   *Shabbat* 105b.

CHAPTER SIX

Can Tragedy Refine Us?

Behold, I refine you, but not as silver;
I try you in the furnace of affliction.
—Isaiah 48:10

We've all heard the tiresome—and sometimes very insensitive—platitudes offered during a time of personal setbacks, or even loss:

"At least she didn't suffer."

"At least you have other children."

"Every cloud has a silver lining."

"Time heals all wounds."

The people who say such things mean well, but when we are burdened with sorrow, the last thing we want to hear is that something good will come out of the tragedy and that we will be its beneficiaries. We are nowhere near ready to hear, let alone feel, such sentiments.

But as we explored in previous chapters, misfortune *can* be a precursor to a positive outcome. Sometimes there *are* silver linings hidden in the dark clouds. Affliction can create the opportunity or the space to help us improve our relationships with other people and with the world—to improve ourselves in ways we wouldn't have imagined before the misfortune befell us. Tragedy has the potential to refine us, to make us better people. However, this process of refinement is not without laborious effort. Becoming a more spiritually developed and emotionally engaged person has tangible benefits, too—it can be a prelude to becoming a happier person.

The refinement process is one in which we separate a material from its impurities, such as lees being filtered from wine or dross skimmed from metal. This filtering process makes the wine or metal finer and purer. People should also want to refine themselves by filtering out their natural impurities, but who is in charge of seeing that they do?

Personal growth of a spiritual nature is difficult. Most people are too comfortable with themselves (even if they know they have problems they should deal with) to take on the challenge. Rare is the person who chooses the challenge of personal growth. But sometimes a tragedy shakes your very character infrastructure to its core, forcing you to review the trajectory of your life. This shake-up provides an unwelcome but potentially life-altering opportunity to rechannel and recalibrate your life—for the good.

Everything that happens to us could and should be an opportunity for growth. A mistake should not be seen as a setback; it should be viewed as a learning experience, with the goal of not repeating the mistake. A wise student who fails a test in school will reflect inwardly: Why did it happen? Did I not study enough? Did I not understand the material well to begin with? Did I party too much the night before the test? An honest assessment will motivate this person to correct the errors, to review the material more thoroughly before the next exam, to pay more attention to absorbing new material when it is new, and definitely to avoid partying the night before an exam!

The benefits of this preparation may extend to others as well. For example, this student may seek out the instructor to ask for help with something that remains unclear or form a study group where several students can share their individual strengths to help one another grasp the material.

If you think that you as an individual can't make a difference, think again

Even an event that is beyond one's control can be an opportunity for growth. Many of the most well-known organizations were launched by those who suffered with a serious condition or found themselves in the wake of a tragedy: Struggling alcoholics Rowland Hazard and Bill Wilson formed Alcoholics Anonymous. Candy Lightner created Mothers Against Drunk Driving (M.A.D.D.) after her daughter was killed by a drunk driver. Nancy Brinker promised her dying sister that she would fight to eradicate breast cancer and then established the Susan G. Komen Foundation. Brady United is a foundation that works to prevent gun violence, named after Jim Brady, press secretary to President Ronald Reagan, who was shot in the head during the March 30, 1981, assassination attempt on the president's life.

In an incredible case of irony, actor Christopher Reeve was thrown from a horse and sustained a permanent spinal-cord injury, which left him paralyzed for the rest of his life. The man who played Superman on screen could not breathe without a ventilator. The Christopher and Dana Reeve Foundation is a leading sponsor of innovative therapies for others suffering paralysis. Its work has helped and given hope to tens of thousands with similar injuries. While Reeve had a wealthy Hollywood network behind him to launch and promote the foundation's work, the founders of AA and M.A.D.D., as well as many other "ordinary" people, did not. Yet they took their personal challenges and built from a grassroots level, eventually making an enormous impact on both individuals and society.

Another example: Rabbi Shlomo Bochner founded the Bonei Olam organization, dedicated to helping infertile couples with treatment that would be otherwise unaffordable to them. This work began through the heartbreak of Rabbi Bochner and his wife, who realized that they would not give birth to their own children. They started to fundraise with small donations to help other couples longing for a child. Slowly, their cause garnered attention and support. Today the organization operates in six countries, and the assistance they have provided has resulted in the births of nearly ten thousand children!

One particularly poignant illustration of transforming personal tragedy into a positive force for good is mentioned by Viktor Frankl in a sequel to his classic book, *Man's Search for Meaning*:[1]

> *A few years after World War II, a woman being examined by a doctor had on a most unusual bracelet. It was*

made of baby teeth all mounted in gold. "A beautiful bracelet," the doctor remarked.

"Yes," the woman answered. "This tooth here belonged to Miriam, this one to Esther, and this one to Samuel...." She mentioned the names of her daughters and sons according to age. "Nine children," she sighed, "and all of them were taken to the gas chambers."

Shocked, the doctor asked, "My God, woman, how can you live with such a bracelet?"

Quietly, the Jewish woman replied, "I am now in charge of an orphanage in Israel."

If you think that you as an individual can't make a difference, think again.

While most people will not have the drive, the resources, or the fortitude to create a foundation or underwrite a hospital wing to commemorate a loss or to help further a cause, anyone can use a loss as a catalyst for growth on a personal level—if you choose to look within and evaluate yourself deeply.

Rochel Leah's death made me a kinder, better person

After my thirty-six-year-old wife passed away suddenly, I was emotionally raw for a very long time. And yet, during that time I also became much more attuned to other people's feelings. By experiencing my own new-found sensitivity, I was able to look back and realize that I had been somewhat callously running roughshod over others. While only thirty-eight years old, I had already been a director of a school with almost four hundred students and eighty employees for ten years, and under the strain of the job, my patience for other people's sensitivities was, shall I say, limited. I had an important job to do, and heaven help the person who kept me from getting it done!

About a year or so after my wife's passing, I realized that my patience was growing, little by little. My children needed me, and I had become more conscious and responsive to their suffering. I began to notice that other people suffered, too. When you feel miserable, you become sensitized to other people's pain. When you have a sprained ankle, you suddenly notice all those other people who are limping. Maybe they had been limping all along, but you may never have noticed them until your own ankle was bundled in a tight compression wrap and you were limping, too. You see that, in fact, some people are worse off than you are. You feel a kinship with them.

Empathy grew within me after our tragedy, and it's still with me. Because of my wife's death, I would like to think I became a kinder, better person.

Do I really have to suffer in order to grow?

Perhaps because I live in California, where we experience earthquakes on a fairly regular basis, I relate to Dr. Kübler-Ross' stages of grief (described in the previous chapter) as reactions to an emotional earthquake. Not all earthquakes damage our homes or make us anxious in the long term, but some do, and some devastatingly so. Some earthquakes cause cosmetic damage that construction "cosmetologists" (such as plasterers, drywall hangers, and painters) can fix. Other earthquakes cause more significant damage: Walls collapse or houses slip off their foundations. In those cases, you need to call in a structural engineer to assess what can be shored up and what needs to be demolished and reconstructed. I see the Kübler-Ross stages of grief as the psychological analogue of the assessment and need for rebuilding after the earthquake.

It is in the last of the stages—acceptance—where there is real growth. When you reach acceptance, you stop spinning your wheels as you had been doing during the previous four phases and come to terms with reality. Those earlier stages are like a car in neutral on a cold day. Your engine needs time to warm up, but you still can't go anywhere until you put the car in gear. The stage of acceptance puts you in "Drive." You can start navigating toward a higher level of emotional awareness and calm.

The same is true when confronting the spiritual impact after a tragedy. Wrenching as it might be, accepting that the trauma you suffered was orchestrated by God for a reason and a purpose provides some solace, even though you have not figured out what that reason or purpose might be. Acceptance can soothe the anger you have toward God and allows you to reconcile again. In fact, after this reconciliation you'll be able to be closer to God than you were before, having survived the stress test of your relationship. This can also be seen as a refinement of your previous relationship with God.

In his book, *Let Us Make Man*,[2] rabbi and psychiatrist Dr. Abraham J. Twerski* wrote about a woman who

---

* **Rabbi Dr. Abraham J. Twerski, MD, 1930–2021:** Psychiatrist and noted author. A scion of the Chernobyl Chasidic dynasty, Rabbi Twerski

spoke about her recovery from alcoholism. She told a harrowing tale of trauma and loss during her many years of a
drinking addiction. When asked how she survived all her
problems, she said:

> I did not really believe in God except as the object for all
> my anger and bitterness. Why are You doing this to me?
> What is it that You want from me? Only now, after eight
> years of sobriety, can I see that God was taking from
> me those things that I did not have the good judgment
> to get rid of by myself. Looking back with a clear mind,
> I can see that the marriage was not in my best interest,
> nor was the job. Now, I have gone back to school and am
> getting my master's degree, which I never would have
> done otherwise. I am now happily remarried, with a re-
> lationship that is far healthier than the other one could
> ever have been.

Rabbi Twerski was profoundly moved by this woman's
story, but he wondered: Does a person really have to suffer to grow and mature? Couldn't there be an alternate
method for achieving the refinement of one's personality and character? He thought that if he had been the one
who designed the world, he would have tried to establish
a painless pathway to growth. But he wrote:

> ... the fact is that I did not design the world, and God
> did. My belief in the infinite wisdom and the benevo-
> lence of God compels me to conclude that, for reasons

---

was a well-known expert in the field of substance abuse. He authored more
than eighty books on self-help and Judaism and was a pioneer in raising
awareness of the dangers of addiction, spousal abuse, and low self-esteem. He served as medical director of the Gateway Rehabilitation Center
in Pittsburgh and as associate professor of psychiatry at the University of
Pittsburgh School of Medicine.

*completely beyond my capacity to understand, there is
no other way to achieve such personality growth.*

*I believe that God's benevolence far surpasses my own,
and as I try to treat my patients with the least painful
effective treatment, [I know that] certainly God would
provide a painless alternative, if that were possible
according to His infinite wisdom.*[3]

We cannot expect that awareness of suffering as a
growth process will significantly diminish our pain, nor
will it necessarily eliminate the anger and the bitterness
that we naturally feel in the first throes of suffering. The
Talmud states, "A person is not culpable for the feelings
he has, even blasphemous ones, when he is suffering."[4]
God does not find fault with those who are unable to endure suffering with equanimity. Rather, we hope that after the acute pain subsides, we will be able to apply our
faith and trust and accept our past suffering as somehow
having been necessary for our spiritual growth.

Perhaps rarest of all is the young person who understands the potential for growth and refinement through
suffering. In 1938, at age seventeen, Edmund N. Carpenter[5] wrote about his goals in life with precocious maturity:

*Before I die, I want to feel a great sorrow. This, perhaps,
of all my wishes will seem the strangest to the reader.
Yet, is it unusual that I should wish to have had a complete life? I want to have lived fully, and certainly sorrow is a part of life. It is my belief that, as in the case of
love, no man has lived until he has felt sorrow. It molds
us and teaches us that there is a far deeper significance
to life than might be supposed if one passed through
this world forever happy and carefree. Moreover, once*

*the pangs of sorrow have slackened, for I do not believe
it to be a permanent emotion, its dregs often leave us
a better knowledge of this world of ours and a better
understanding of humanity.*[6]

(Carpenter would eventually win the Bronze Star for
his service in World War II, graduate from Harvard Law
School, become the president of a law firm, marry, and
have six children and fifteen grandchildren.)

Can prayer turn you into a different person?

Prayer can be an important component of a suffering person's pathway to greater understanding and sensitivity.
We commonly pray to entreat God for the things we need
or want. But the Hebrew word for prayer is *tefillah*, which
means to connect. The Jewish concept of prayer is to first
"Know before Whom you stand,"[7] through introspection
and submission, "meditating on God's grandeur and man's
insignificance."[8] That brings a person to the ideal frame of
mind for prayer, of connecting with God, and being wor-
thy of having one's requests be heard.

The Mishnah* says: "One should only get up and begin to pray from an approach of gravity and submission."[9]
Earlier generations of Jews had a tradition to prepare for

---

* **Mishnah:** The first authoritative work of Jewish law that was codi-
fied in writing. The Mishnah contains the oral traditions that were passed
down from teacher to student; it supplements, clarifies, and systematizes
the commandments of the Torah. Due to the continual persecution of the
Jewish people, it became increasingly difficult to guarantee that these traditions would not be forgotten. Rabbi Yehudah the Nasi therefore redacted
the Mishnah at the end of the second century. It serves as the foundation
for the Talmud.

formal prayer by meditating for one hour beforehand. Only afterward did they feel that their hearts were focused sufficiently toward their Father in heaven and pray. Prayer requires focus. The concepts of "gravity and submission" may sound forbidding, but during prayer, you are a participant and a petitioner. And you are addressing your "Father in heaven."

This raises an interesting question. If we accept that everything that happens to us is directed by God, including being struck by illness, just how does someone who is ill pray to be healed? In a memorable article, Rabbi Zev Schostak offers a valuable perspective:

> *Prayer changes the patient and elevates him to a higher spiritual level, where he may become worthy of God's blessings and miracles... . Through sickness and suffering, intercessory prayer, and, most importantly, genuine repentance, a patient may undergo a spiritual transformation and become a different person. Indeed, God did not change His mind. His harsh decree was made against the patient's former self and not against whom he has become—a renewed and truly transformed individual.*[10]

From Rabbi Schostak's explanation, it can be understood that the person who is praying for health is, in effect, saying, "You, God, have decreed that I should be sick, and I am turning to You. I faced myself and my reality, and I reviewed my own state of affairs. I recognized that my life is not as it should be, and I am prepared, whether You're making a deal or not, to transform myself."

That is what prayer is all about. God knows He has

your attention and is ready to respond to the new you with a clean slate.

Pain is inevitable, but suffering is optional

While tragedy can refine us, it doesn't have to define us. This, too, is a choice that requires concerted effort. When we, the parents, were searching for a suitable marriage partner for one of our children in the customary courtship practice of many Orthodox Jews, we knew of two ideal candidates. Deciding which one to pursue was difficult. Both were from large families, and, as it happened, both had lost their fathers a few years earlier. Therefore, we focused on the mothers, the would-be mother-in-law of our child. One of the mothers appeared burdened and lugubrious. The other, while also burdened, had nevertheless retained her intrinsic joyfulness. This was the tiebreaker.

If you see your challenging circumstance as "random," you are likely to view yourself as a victim. "Why me?" you cry, believing there can be no satisfying answer to this question. But if you see your circumstance not as happenstance but as planned—albeit for reasons beyond your understanding—you have the tools to help yourself cope.

In my community, I'm often called upon to help people write the Hebrew epitaph for their beloved's gravestone. Often, the deceased had gone through a period of suffering from illness and/or treatment, whether it was from cancer, chemotherapy, kidney dialysis, etc. There are choices among Hebrew expressions that one can inscribe on a gravestone that refer to the deceased's suffering. One expression is that the deceased "shouldered their suffering with love." An alternate phrase is that the deceased was "refined by their suffering."

I ask the members of the immediate family who had spent many nights at their loved one's bedside to ask themselves, "Please consider, was it her final suffering, difficult as it was for her and for the family, which defined your mother? Do you want your own children and grandchildren, when they visit Bubby's grave, to think about the last year when she was so ill, or do you want her to be remembered as a proud loving mother and dignified grandmother who lived a wholesome and happy life?" (Now, when a person suffered from a prolonged chronic illness, that's a different story, and I do not judge.)

I hope that's a lesson for all survivors. Every life includes periodic misfortunes, but that doesn't mean life is not good, nor does it mean that you have a problem with God. If pain and suffering are part of an overarching positive plan, it may take months or years to gain perspective and see the revealed plan at work. When you can see the purpose, it reassures you that the "bad" was not completely bad.

Are you ready for a reboot to HumanBeing 2.0?

A few years prior to Rochel Leah's passing, and unrelated to that sudden, shocking event, I went through a difficult stretch and read a book by psychiatrist Dr. Frederic Flach, *The Secret Strength of Depression.*[11] The thesis of the book is that when a person is depressed, soul-searching is required to define and address the obvious problem. In my own personal terminology, I would say that depression is a malfunction of the system that requires a person to do a complete overhaul. This requires disassembling and inspecting one's moving parts, repairing the parts that are repairable, discarding and replacing those that no longer work with shiny new parts that will make it all work better. Once all these repairs, discards, and introduction of new parts are put together, you are ready for a reboot, to HumanBeing 2.0.

Simply stated: If you continue to think as you thought and do as you did, you'll have what you had. If you want to have something different and better, you'll have to think and do differently.

In the human analogue, the "parts" are one's ego, values, proclivities, habits, old ways of thinking, and assumptions. It is hard work to evaluate them and to let go of those habits, ways of thinking, values, etc. that no longer serve you well and may have never served you well. Working with a caring clergy member, a spiritual mentor, or a good therapist can help jump-start this work. You can learn how to take a deeper look inside yourself, work to understand yourself better, and begin again in a new and healthier way. Coasting through life may seem good, but you'll always just be skimming the surface, never digging down to discover life's deepest meaning. And as your life circumstances change, you may find that a reboot is necessary. And as we now see, sometimes the "bad" things that prompt the reboot end up being for our good.

After a medical procedure or surgery, the pain of recovery is inevitable and undoubtedly real. It's a reminder that something that was amiss in your body has now been repaired. Your future health will be the better for it.

We have to distinguish pain from suffering. Pain is part of the human condition and comes from the Creator. Suffering is inflicted by human beings on themselves. Pain usually has an end point, while suffering can go on indefinitely. Pain is inevitable, while suffering is optional. When does pain morph into suffering? If someone hurts you physically or emotionally, the attack results in pain. You acknowledge that you're injured or that your feelings are hurt. The physical pain will recede in due time and may eventually disappear. But if you keep ruminating on the experience, or if you keep thinking, "I can't believe what that lowlife did to me!" then a month later, or a year later, you may still feel the emotional sting from that insult. That kind of suffering is optional, because you are choosing to hold onto it. We can *choose* to suffer for a long time from insult, misfortune, or from poor health, but that is a choice. A better choice is to turn our painful experiences to something positive by transforming them into something from which we can grow.

Those who exercise regularly know that the mild pain from exercising is a blessing because it's a part of growth. Muscles grow when they're stressed and challenged. Likewise, we grow from our challenges even when they are painful. This is how we mature and become wise. If we resist these opportunities and refuse to engage with life's challenges, we risk remaining immature, unfulfilled, emotionally stuck, and frequently sad.

When my wife passed away suddenly, I didn't have the

luxury of descending into a depression and not getting out
of bed for weeks. I had to rise to the occasion and focus on
the tasks before me. So I did what I needed to do. It took
a few years until I had the luxury of thinking about myself, and that is when I realized what a steep price I had
paid for that delay in processing my loss psychologically
and emotionally. However, given my circumstances at the
time, forging ahead was the right thing to do.

God has put us all here for a purpose

At the same time, I was fortunate in that I had a robust
weltanschauung, a foundational perspective on life that
helped me move forward. Right there in the hospital,
shortly after the doctor made his pronouncement, I remember thinking, *Life as I have known it has changed forever. This is my opportunity to put everything that I believe
in, and everything that I've learned and taught until now,
into action. Am I up for it?* I was then thirty-eight years
old. My belief in Jewish theology and that God runs the
world didn't allow me to see this calamity as a chance
event, or that I had drawn the short straw. I saw this as
a deliberate event coming from God. I did not know then
nor now why God chose me and my family for this trial,
but I didn't doubt that this was God's plan.

When a tragedy occurs and its pain is inflicted on
many people, those people are not collateral damage.[12]
This event, this pain, was intended for each of those people, too. When my wife passed away, each member of our
immediate and extended family was affected differently:
me, every one of my children—from the fourteen-year-old

to the sixteen-month-old twins—and my wife's mother and siblings. This also held true for her students and friends on whom she had profound influence. Each of us experienced a different type of loss, and our lives are different today because of that event. Ideally, we have each grown through that challenge.

In my heart, I knew that everything is from God and everything is for the good, even when it *wasn't* good. When I became a widower, I was comforted by the idea that God put me on earth for a purpose; I just needed to keep working for that purpose. I didn't tell myself that everything was good. Clearly, I was wrestling with huge, relentless challenges. I won't sugarcoat that time of my life. I was hurting, and it was not good.

Just as we can grow from stress, whether psychological or physical, we can also grow from pain. We can embrace an attitude that will help us find the determination to find purpose in our pain. This does not in the slightest ease the immediate ache, but it does infuse us with strength to endure, knowing there is meaning in everything that happens. This knowledge should strengthen us to have hope in the future.

Some of you might think it's a bit far-fetched to think that every person can find purpose in their pain. After all, we are all so different in character, nature, and even psychological resilience. How can it be realistic for someone to face a crisis or calamity with calm reflection and a philosophical outlook when their emotions are turbulent, even raging?

These questions miss the point. We cannot deny our

emotional responses. We cannot successfully adopt a mind-over-matter philosophy during a crisis. What we can do, however, is anchor ourselves on the bedrock of *emunah*, the faith that God is really the One Who runs our world and Whose intentions are only for the good. Inculcating this belief is beyond philosophy or emotions. It goes to our very core, and it is an idea that is equally accessible and applicable to everyone, regardless of their nature or character.

If we were capable of refining or purifying our souls without tragedy to guide us, we might be more like angels than human beings. However, angels are static—they never change. Human beings are dynamic—we can grow and change beyond anything we might have imagined.

Think about this: It takes a lot of pressure to turn carbon into diamonds. If we can withstand the pressure, we will shine as never before.

Chapter Summary: *There is no sugarcoating the intense pain of tragedy. It is raw and primal. Even when we are ready to understand that we can grow from the process of finding purpose in the pain, the pain does not disappear. We can find meaning and hope in our situation, and this discovery may even motivate us to work on behalf of others who have suffered as we have. Releasing our anger toward God over our tragedy can open the doors for reconciliation with Him, which will also bring much-needed calm. Ultimately, prolonged suffering is an unhelpful choice. Pain can refine us, but it should not define us.*

Endnotes:

1   Viktor Frankl, *Man's Search for Ultimate Meaning: An Introduction to Logotherapy* (New York: Basic Books, 2000).

2   Rabbi Dr. Abraham J. Twerski, *Let Us Make Man: Self-Esteem Through Jewishness* (Lakewood, NJ: CIS Publishers, 1987).

3   Ibid.

4   *Bava Batra* 16b.

5   American war hero, attorney, father (1921–2008). This excerpt was from an op-ed, "Before I Die … ," *Wall Street Journal,* February 6, 2010.

6   This 1938 essay was republished as *The Wall Street Journal* op-ed "Before I Die," by Edmund N. Carpenter, 2/6/10.

7   *Brachot* 28b.

8   Rema (Rabbi Moshe Isserlis) *Shulchan Aruch, Orach Chayim* 98; Rabbi Schneur Zalman of Liadi, *Shulchan Aruch Harav*, ad loc.

9   *Brachot* 5:1.

10 Rabbi Zev Schostak, "Final Confessions: Dialogues in a Jewish Geriatric Center," *Jewish Action,* Vol. 53, no. 3 (Summer 5753/1993).

11 Frederic Flach, M.D., *The Secret Strength of Depression* (Long Island City, NY: The Hatherleigh Company, Ltd., 2009).

12 Numbers 16:22 in Rashi's commentary

CHAPTER SEVEN

Is Suffering a Test of Faith?

My child, do not despise God's discipline, and do not loathe His reproof; for God admonishes the one He loves, even as a father corrects the son in whom he delights.
—*Proverbs 3:11–12*

In earlier chapters, we've discovered that the Jewish approach to understanding why severe troubles befall us is that they could be meant to refine our character or punish us for wrongdoing. But there are other legitimate approaches, as well. In this chapter, we'll examine the possibility that God is really doing something else altogether: He is testing us.

Most of us don't like to be tested, even about what we know: not at school, not at work, not at the Department of Motor Vehicles. We're even less pleased when we think a close friend, relative, or partner has set us up to test our loyalty or fidelity. We ask ourselves: How can someone I love doubt me enough to resort to subterfuge?

It's terrible when you or people you love are beset with troubles through absolutely no fault of their own. We're even distressed by the apparent injustices that befall upstanding people we don't know. "These are good people!" we cry out. "They don't deserve to suffer this way!"

Jews believe that God tests His people to see if they will stick together and remain a unit that maintains its traditional allegiance to Him. God may test a family to ascertain whether they will keep their covenant with Him. And God may test an individual to find out if the person retains his faith even when tragedy strikes and He seems to be absent and not providing any help.

Job, the quintessential innocent sufferer

The Mishnah says that God tested Abraham ten times.[1] The ultimate, most grueling test was the *Akedah*, the binding of his beloved son Isaac as a sacrifice: How far was Abraham willing to go to prove that he put God first in his life? We believe that when God tests us, it's because He knows we have the strength to pass that test.

We're by now familiar with Job, the quintessential model of innocent suffering. The very first verse of the biblical book named for him tells us that Job was *wholesome and upright; he feared God and shunned evil*. Nevertheless, he undergoes a test of his faithfulness. When God tells the Satan (usually translated as the Adversary) that Job is a fine and faithful person, the Satan counters with critique that minimizes Job's piety and gives a base reason for it: *For have You not set a protective wall around him, his household, and all he has? You have blessed the work of his hands, and his possessions have multiplied in the land. But reach out Your hand and strike all that he has*, the Satan challenges, *and he will curse You to Your face.*[2] God picks up the gauntlet, putting Job under the Satan's power.

In short order, Job is stripped of his livestock, his possessions, and his ten children. Then the Satan (with God's consent) afflicts Job *with severe boils from the soles of his feet to the top of his head.* His wife, believing Job has nothing left to live for, suggests that he *blaspheme God, and die!* But Job refuses to curse God or even blame Him: *Shall we accept only the good from God, and not accept the bad?*[3]

> *Then three of Job's friends heard of all the bad that had befallen him ... and they gathered together and came to mourn with him and to comfort him. They saw him from the distance and didn't recognize him [for his appearance was transformed by his suffering]. They raised their voices and cried, and they tore their clothes and threw dust over their heads heavenward. They sat with Job on the ground for seven days and seven nights and no one said a word to him, for they saw that his suffering was excruciating.*[4]

For the next thirty-five chapters, the friends try to puzzle out why God has visited such suffering on Job. A recurrent theme in these chapters is that Job's friends imply that since God *must* be right, ergo, Job must be sinful—a contention that Job categorically rejects. Another recurring theme throughout the book is Job's considerable rancor over good people being made to suffer while the wicked prosper.

Close to the book's finale, God speaks to Job for the first time, in two poetic and abstract chapters:

> *God then responded to Job from out of the whirlwind and said:*
>
> *"Who is this who gives murky counsel with words without knowledge?*

"Gird your loins like a warrior, and I will ask you, and you will inform Me.

"Where were you when I laid the earth's foundation? Tell, if you know understanding! Who set its dimensions?—if you know—or who stretched a [surveyor's] line over it? Into what are its bases sunken, or who laid its cornerstone?

"... Have you penetrated the hidden depths of the sea or gone to plumb the deep? Were the gates of death revealed to you? Have you seen the gates of the shadow of death?

"Have you contemplated up to the wide expanses of the world? Tell, if you know it all! What is the path where the light dwells? And darkness, where is its place, that you may take it to its boundary, that you may understand the paths of its home? Did you know when you would be born, and [how] many are the number of your days?[5]

"... Is it by your wisdom that the hawk hovers, spreads its wings toward the south? Is it by your command that the eagle soars, or makes his nest on high, dwelling and lodging in the clefts of rocks, upon rocky cliff and tower, from there he searches for food, his eyes look out to the distance?"[6]

In these chapters, God reminds Job that He is the Creator and in charge of everything that happens in nature and to human beings. Until Job possesses the abilities that God has, it is futile for him to try to figure out why God does anything. Job's final avowal to God is: *Behold, I am deficient; what can I answer You? I place my hand against my mouth! I spoke once and I will not speak up again. I will say no more.*[7] The long-suffering Job concedes that God's actions transcend all human understanding, repudiating his doubts and apologizing for all his questions. This is when God restores Job's fortunes.

Job's story is one of the most poetic and fascinating books of the Bible, and it is among the most difficult to understand. It may also be the most dynamic book in the Bible, because the reader observes its characters—Job and his friends—deliberating over life's greatest questions of right and wrong, and reward and suffering, as they try to figure out why bad things happen to innocent people. And when God finally gives His answer, it puts the questioning mortals in their place. Paraphrasing God, the answer is: "You can't understand why I do what I do, not because you're too insignificant to know, but because I am unknowable. It's not like 'I'm the teacher, and you're the student,' who have some commonality. It is that 'I'm the Creator and you're a mortal, a creature; you are dimensional and I am dimensionless.'"

God is pointing out the unbridgeable chasm between Him and mere mortals. Why should anyone even think they would be able to understand how and why God does what He does? It takes an awful lot of suffering before Job accepts that it is part of God's plan. At that point, he realizes not only that he doesn't need to know why, but he also recognizes that he can never truly understand God's decisions and actions. Only with this final acceptance does Job achieve full commitment to God.

The Talmud[8] contains eight differing opinions on the era when Job lived and when his story occurred. A ninth

Sage asserted that Job's story was only a parable and Job was an apocryphal character. This vagueness, unique among biblical figures, supports the thesis that the book of Job is metaphorical. In other words, the challenge of human suffering is universal and timeless. It cannot be identified with any particular period, person, or circumstance.

Nachmanides takes the view that Job was not afflicted because the Satan offered his challenge, but because God chose to test Job's faith. In bringing Job to the Satan's attention, God expected that the Satan would devise several ways to carry out these tests. The Satan and the angels are completely opposite except in one fundamental respect: Neither has free choice. They can only carry out God's will. This means that the Satan had no means by which he could challenge God and initiate the tests on his own.

(Job's suffering may have been especially meaningful to Nachmanides, who lived at a time when his native Spain was imposing severe laws against Jews. Nachmanides was forced to engage in a religious disputation* with a Dominican friar and was subsequently expelled from Spain.)

This view of Job's tests contrasts strongly with Nachmanides' commentary on Abraham, whom God tested repeatedly, culminating in His order to bring his son Isaac to Mount Moriah as a sacrifice. Nachmanides sees Abraham's climactic test not as a test of his *faith* but of his *righteousness*:

---

* The disputation at Barcelona took place in July 1263 in four sessions between Nachmanides and Friar Pablo Christiani, a Jewish apostate.

"When God knows that a righteous person will act according to His will but still seeks [that person to act with] their *own* righteousness, He will command him to a test," Nachmanides says. He adds, "Every test in the Torah is for the good of the one being tested."[9]

God's angel calls out to Abraham just before he is about to sacrifice his son, ordering him to stop. God knows that Abraham, a righteous man, would obey God's instruction to *offer* Isaac as a sacrifice. But herein God's plan was revealed: God never intended that Abraham go through with it, which would counter His promise that He would make Abraham's progeny *exceedingly numerous.*[10] Nachmanides adds[11] that Abraham's reward for his righteousness is that his descendants will never be destroyed and will be redeemed.

Similarly, we read in Psalms, *God tries the righteous.*[12] Like the potter in the marketplace demonstrating the strength of his vessels—mentioned in a previous chapter[13]—God tests both Abraham and Job, wanting to demonstrate that their *potential* righteousness is in fact *actual* righteousness.

Can we see the bigger picture?

Since God only poses challenges to those He knows can pass the test, why test them at all? For what purpose? Because by passing the tests, they have actualized their potential and discovered more of their own abilities. Like a good coach, God may push us further than we think we can go. And when we do, we have grown. We have a better appreciation for the extent of our endurance and faith.

If we can identify with this idea, then when we encounter a challenge, we will say to ourselves, "If I couldn't handle this, God would not burden me with it. Therefore, I know I can do it, and I will." Or we can remember the aphorism, "Whether you think you can, or you think you can't—you're right."

The ability to pass the tests of faith in your life depends on being able to step away from yourself and see the bigger picture—the world as it exists beyond your own experience. God's first instruction to Abraham was, *Go for yourself, from your land, from your birthplace, and from your father's house to the land I will show you.*[14] This was Abraham's first test. When you look at the mirror in the morning, you see yourself and only yourself. The image you see doesn't tell you much about yourself beyond what you look like (which you already knew), and perhaps whether you've had a good night's sleep. To experience life, you have to turn away from the mirror, look out the window, and walk out the door. The further you travel and the more of the landscape you take in, the more readily you can handle what life throws at you.

We meet many tests of faith during our lifetime: small ones that challenge our comforts, larger ones that challenge our principles, and cataclysmic events that strike at the core of our being, forcing us to ask, "Who am I *really*?" Every test, minor or major, requires us to look at life from a perspective beyond ourselves, even if seeing that new vantage point makes us uncomfortable. This is what stimulates character growth and, eventually, maturity. The greater the test, the larger the picture we need to take in.

Sometimes, we face tests that put our lives on the line, in accordance with God's instruction in the *Shema,* the central Jewish creed proclaiming God's oneness, to love Him *with all your soul.*[15] This means that in certain rare cases, we must do what may seem like giving up our very souls in defense of that love.

The Previous Lubavitcher Rebbe, Rabbi Yosef Yitzchak Schneersohn, faced such a test. In the summer of 1920, just a few months after his saintly father's passing, the Rebbe was leading the morning *Shacharit* service and saying the Mourner's *Kaddish,* as is the established practice for a son to honor his parent. However, this was during the Bolshevik revolution, when public displays of religion were under constant assault. Here is an abbreviated account of what happened that day:

> On that morning three members of the Cheka, the secret police (and precursor to the KGB), rushed into the synagogue, loaded rifles in hand, belts hung with a pair of revolvers and Cossack knives. They wore copper helmets, and their faces were aflame. They approached and summoned me to a so-called "meeting." Two of the members were Jews, and I had helped one of them by loaning him money and helping him get a job in a cigarette factory. The two Jewish members demanded that I remove my tallit and tefillin on the spot. I refused and completed my prayers.
>
> Afterward, they led me to a large chamber—the "courtyard of death." They surrounded me in the manner that those accused of treason against the regime are led. I sat at the foot of a long table, with fifteen men on each side

and two others at the head of the table. The three guards continued to surround me.

This was a Communist inquisition, conducted in Russian, against the practice of Judaism and of Chasidic practices in particular. To their questions, I replied in Yiddish that, just as I had on prior "visits" to the Cheka, I steadfastly refused to budge from my principles. While I was still speaking, a "committee member" on the right side pointed a revolver at me. "This toy does away with 'principles.' Fear of it has opened many a mouth. Also the dumb have become talkative before it."

"You are utterly mistaken," I said. "This toy impresses only the cowardly atheist, who has but a single world and many gods.... . But as for us, who have but a single God and believe in two worlds, the toy that you are brandishing not only fails to frighten, it makes no impression whatsoever."[16]

Having faith in God is not only based on emotion. Having faith is also consistent with critical thinking. God does not expect us to pass His tests of our faith by stifling our minds or our ability to reason. God would never issue a commandment that defies logic or reason, such as, "Thou shall accept that two plus two equals five," because He knows that our God-given reason will prove otherwise. We can force ourselves to *think* the words *two plus two equals five*, but we cannot *reason* that two plus two truly equals five.

Codifiers of Jewish law have argued that the commandment to love God seems not to be viable: How can anyone be commanded to love? "If I feel love, then I love," they say. "If I don't love, I don't. You can command me to do a deed, such as to fast on Yom Kippur. That I can accept. I may not want to fast, but fasting is a concrete action—actually an inaction!—not an emotion, so I can fast simply because You commanded me. But when You command me to love, what if I don't love?"

The answer will sound familiar to anyone who has been in couples' therapy, when the couple tells the counselor that they have stopped loving each other. Good marriage counselors will tell them this: Love doesn't come out of nowhere. It is borne out of consistent loving actions: the emotion follows the action. This is how you can work to develop, or redevelop, the love.

And so, God might say, "You learned how to fast, and you can learn to love Me, as well. To know me is to love Me. You will find me in the Torah. Study the Torah, and you'll get to know Me, and you'll find out that I'm lovable!" As King David instructed his son Solomon, *Know the God of your father and serve Him with a wholesome heart.*[17]

Jews have a built-in need for spiritual nourishment. God intended that this need be fed by the Torah, and, historically, it's easy to see that Jews have always been spiritual seekers. Unfortunately, many Jews have sought spirituality outside the framework of Torah, such as in Eastern religions (which have their own sources in Judaism), political movements, and other philosophies. It is rather remarkable that so many secular Jews have found their way back to immersive Torah study and observance over the past two generations, especially at a time when the lures of secular society have grown stronger.

Loving God and struggling with God are not mutually exclusive

The same reasoning applies to righteousness and justice. We aren't supposed to turn off our common sense and say, "We're supposed to be righteous and just, but if something awful happens and God doesn't seem to be righteous and just, that's okay, because He's God." As we have explored thus far, this categorically is not what Judaism is about.

We have seen many examples from the Torah—Abraham and Moses immediately leap to mind. Their faith and belief in God is unshakable, but they were not only permitted but obligated to ask God, "Why did You allow this tragedy to occur? Where is Your sense of justice? Where is Your practice of justice?" *Am I the one who is not perceiving the situation correctly, or is it You, God?*

The real challenge is to be patient in finding out the answer. Sometimes the answer does not come through foresight but becomes clearer in hindsight. It could take a lifetime; in the case of historical catastrophes, it could take centuries.

The name of the Jewish people, Israel, means to wrestle with God.[18] The Jewish obligation is to struggle throughout life with this question: *Why do bad things happen to good people?* Loving God and struggling with God are not mutually exclusive. Ideally, when suffering comes, you say to yourself, "I believe in God and love God. Therefore, I believe His actions are just, but when His actions don't appear to be just, I have permission to challenge Him. I don't lose faith. I still trust in God, but I can trust in Him knowing that I have a problem with Him. After all, God probably has some problems with me."

My nephew Rabbi Binyamin Wolff was a rabbi in Hanover, Germany, where he and his wife, Shterna, made a dynamic team for over fifteen years, building up a thriving Jewish community for those who would otherwise have been estranged from God and religion. Tragically, he passed away at forty-three years old, leaving behind a wife and eight children. Displaying superhuman determination, his widow decided to carry on their work on her own. Her impact on the community has been so notable that in 2022, the German political journal *Rundblick Niedersachsen* presented Shterna with the "Lower Saxony Woman of the Year" award for her work leading Chabad activities in Hanover and Lower Saxony. When asked in an interview, "Are you still a believer?" she answered: "It is a struggle. I have many questions, but I do not have doubts."[19]

We aren't supposed to worship God with faith alone. Just as intelligence is very important in serving God but insufficient by itself, faith, too, is fundamentally important, but also insufficient in itself. We need to work with both. It's our responsibility to develop a philosophy for ourselves—a personal, integrated outlook on life based on learning and values. This philosophy, or *weltanschauung*, needs to be substantial enough to filter down into our consciousness, so that somewhere along the line it will have an impact on your day-to-day attitudes. It's a good thing to have when you need it.

God gives everyone the tools that are appropriate for

154 WHY GOD WHY?

them, tools uniquely tailored for their individual life missions that will help them navigate life positively. I taught that concept for the sixteen years I served as a rabbi before I lost my wife. Not until my wife died, however, did I understand that concept from the inside.

Knowing it, digesting it, and realizing its truth is very different when you've experienced a devastating turn of events. But I had centuries of Jewish history and theology to support me, as well as my own developed *weltanschauung*. I understand that it's much harder to make sense of tragic events without a religious tradition and a personal philosophy to fall back on; that's why I'm writing this book! Often, I don't understand why certain things happen, but I have an all-powerful God to lean on, the One Who is in charge of everything. I'd rather put my trust in the One Who is all powerful than in a God Who is weak and impotent, unable to manage His creation.

The good rabbi's folly

As discussed earlier, perhaps the most popular book in recent years about coping with tragedy is the book I referenced earlier, Rabbi Harold Kushner's *When Bad Things Happen to Good People*. The book, published in 1981, still retains enormous currency among Jews and non-Jews alike.

Rabbi Kushner and his wife tragically lost their son Aaron Zev at age fourteen to an incurable degenerative genetic disease, progeria, also known as Hutchinson-Gilford syndrome, which causes rapid and premature aging. He was diagnosed as a small child, and they suffered with him as his condition deteriorated. The pain that Rabbi Kushner endured as a result of that loss prompted him to write his book to help others also coping with unexpected and devastating loss.

I walk a fine line here, because as a rabbi who has been in the "consolation business" for almost half a century, the last thing I would ever do is judge the feelings of a person who endured the tragedy that Rabbi Kushner experienced. At the same time, I cannot refrain from pointing out that the response he offered readers is inadequate, and I will go even further and state that it is not an authentically Jewish response, or even a religious one. I understand that Rabbi Kushner's intentions were to process his own loss and try to alleviate the suffering of others. If his answers offer solace of a kind to readers, well and good. But his philosophy is absolutely at odds with the Judaism that our Torah teaches and our rabbis have understood and explained for thousands of years.

Let me explain.

Rabbi Kushner's book, however well-meaning, sets its readers on a path toward minimizing the power, effectiveness, and total control over the universe that God possesses. It strikes me as an easier path to tread when we claim that God is not responsible for bad things that happen. This approach allows us to believe that tragedies could not come from God, which makes it easier to see God as a totally benevolent Creator. However, it's a much more nuanced way of thinking when we are able to recognize that God *is* all-powerful and accept that reality requires us to come to terms with an outcome that we did not choose, but one that God directed or allowed.

God is not a celestial therapist

Rabbi Kushner's thesis is that God is, as he phrases it, "powerless"—that God does not and cannot intervene in human affairs to avert tragedy and suffering. At most, according to Rabbi Kushner's book, God offers us His Divine comfort and expresses His Divine anger when horrible things happen to people, but God, in the face of tragedy, is impotent. "The most God can do," Kushner eloquently proclaims, "is to stand on the side of the victim; not the executioner." Kushner further asserts that "the purpose of religion is that it should make us feel good about ourselves," and if it doesn't, it has failed in its mission.

The traditional Jewish thinking of thousands of years has differed fundamentally from this understanding. It is not the purpose of religion to make us feel good about ourselves. We are not the center of the universe; God is. If there is a God, our central mission is to find Him, get to know Him, and serve Him. This lifelong exploratory journey *is* the destination, and it can be truly fulfilling and, dare I say, in its own way, exciting. God is not the celestial therapist whose role is to make us feel good about ourselves. Feeling good about ourselves is a by-product of a life lived well and purposefully, with God as our ballast and compass, helping us to steer through its storms without keeling over. A life well lived often means being bruised and then healing from life's inevitable challenges.

If Kushner's view is correct, then renounce the members of the clergy as charlatans and discard the prayer books as offering only a placebo when true medicine is required. Throw away the Psalms as dealing in false-hoods. Excise "Thank God" from our discourse. If we can't appeal to Him to help us because He is incapable, why should we thank Him when things go right? There is a certain intellectual dishonesty to this. As Job admonished his wife, *Shall we accept only the good from God, and not accept the bad?*

Even Kushner acknowledges this dichotomy. When asked in an interview, "You argue that it is simply wrong to blame God for the bad luck, and yet you are perfectly prepared to praise God for the good. How do you reconcile that?" He carefully replied: "Walter Kaufmann[20] calls it 'religious gerrymandering'—that is, you draw the lines for your definition of God to include certain things and exclude others.[21] Gerrymandering is often dishonest in drawing political boundaries, and it is always dishonest in drawing religious boundaries.

In the same interview, Kushner acknowledged that there are only two possibilities to understanding tragedy: God's will or bad luck. Kushner chooses bad luck. I don't find this thesis comforting at all. In Kushner's view, God doesn't run the world. We are therefore hapless victims of chance, nihilism, or evildoers. A neutered God is there to comfort us when the gods of chance turn against us.

Human suffering cannot be meaningless and purpose-less, as Kushner suggests. Shouldn't it be eminently obvi-ous that if life itself has meaning, then suffering must also have meaning?

What does it mean to live by our faith, and why is it important?

When Jews say the *Shema* prayer, tradition dictates that we cover our eyes with our hand. This gesture can be an aid to concentration because we are supposed to pronounce the *Shema* with focus and intensity. Covering our eyes also allows us to focus much more acutely on the "listening" that the *Shema* intends. It has been said that sometimes we cover our eyes because what may be happening in the world is so painful that we can't look. But just because something is painful doesn't mean that God is not its author.

God does not expect us to live by faith alone. In the big picture, Judaism understands that faith needs to be nurtured so that it filters down into one's consciousness. How can this be achieved?

Just as a diamond must be polished to bring out its sparkle and a sapling must be watered to grow tall and strong, faith must be nurtured. The verse, *The righteous one lives by his faith*[22] emphasizes that we are to *live by* faith, which is distinct from just *having* faith. Faith is abstract and peripheral, and we constantly need to develop it so as to bridge the gap between having faith and living by faith. We can do this through a daily mindful focus on God, learning Torah, and the consistent practice of *mitzvot* and prayer.

When we achieve this level, we can *experience* our faith that the unknowable God is actually in charge. We can *trust* that God is good and wants to and will help His children. At the same time, Jewish tradition teaches us to be realistic. What does this mean?

Being realistic doesn't mean, *God, You stick to Your business and I'll stick to mine.* It means, *God, I will make a life in the world that is consistent with the values and laws You provided as a framework so that Your governance can have practical applications.* This means that we approach every role in our lives—professional and personal—with honor, honesty, and integrity. Every act should be consistent with our faith.

Faith and challenge are not mutually exclusive. In fact, we need both because we have a relationship with the *two* aspects of God: One is the God Who transcends His relationship with the world. The second is the God *in* the physical world, the God Who experiences the stresses and restrictions of the world. As many verses in the Psalms and daily prayers attest to the idea that, *I [God] am with him in his travail.*[23]

We learn from Jewish teachings that each aspect of God is real and present, and, therefore, that we can communicate with God at any moment, in good times or bad.

Consider the mature child who knows her father loves her and that her father is much wiser than she is. At the same time, this daughter knows she cannot *really* understand her father. When her father challenges her, she tries to understand why. Her maturity allows her to see that when her understanding falters, her trust kicks in, so that she never feels abandoned. Can we be as mature in our relationship with God, our Heavenly Father, as the daughter is in this example with her flesh-and-blood father here on earth?

Part of God's readiness to test us is a desire to be part of every aspect of our lives. This does not make God like some celestial "helicopter parent," intruding into our lives. No. God stays actively involved in our lives to support us, not to control us. We see this easily in the morning blessings of each day.

We thank God for our body's functioning; for the soul that was restored to us upon awakening; for our ability to distinguish between darkness and light; for our ability to see with our eyes; to straighten up when we get out of bed; and for providing for all our needs. In these statements of faith that we recite in our daily morning blessings, we practice our awareness and appreciation for God's loving engagement with us. Even when our health is less than ideal, when we have aches and pains and worries, offering these blessings helps us start our day with gratitude for what we *do* have—a mindset that can only support any other physical healing we may need.

Have we relegated God to a designated compartment of our lives?

It is human nature to compartmentalize our lives. This can unfortunately include sticking God into one of the compartments, retrieving Him from His compartment only at particular "God times," such as life-cycle events, Shabbat, and festivals. When a tragedy occurs, we are angry with God: Hasn't He violated the agreement by breaking out of His compartment? Who asked Him to pervade every aspect of our lives? It's easy to think, "God, I love You, but You're messing with the boundaries. You've invaded my life and made it miserable."

We often forget that God wants to be connected with us. He wants to have a home in the world where we live. More than that, He wants us to invite Him in to live in our homes, sharing everything. So, when something bad happens, it's a test of how much a person has detached from God. The person who keeps God behind a barrier or relegated to one room of the house is upset, perhaps even outraged, when He breaches the barrier and sits down on the new couch in the living room.

The person who connects with God all the time understands that God has chosen him or her to handle a tough, even devastating, situation as part of an ultimate commitment. There is no doctrine in Judaism stating that God *will* put everyone to a rigorous test, but if we are put to the test, the Celestial Potter has confidence that we will not shatter when dropped.

The Torah tells us to "choose life," and Jewish law is designed with this in mind. However, Jews are required to be willing to give up their lives when facing a test over one of Judaism's three cardinal sins: repudiating the One God and accepting a foreign one; murder; and sexual immorality (e.g., incest, adultery, bestiality). Throughout history, countless thousands have followed this Torah imperative. We saw this on a large scale during the Crusades, when Rhineland Jews took their lives rather than spurn our God. We saw it again during the Spanish Inquisition. It even goes as far back as the original story of Chanukah, as told in Josephus' *The History of the Jewish War Against the Romans,* when Chanah's seven sons∗ died at the hands of the Syrian-Greek ruler rather than bowing to his idol.

These Jews knew what they were living for and, therefore, what they were willing to die for. Do we each know what we are living for?

The Jewish people have demonstrated the collective ability to keep faith in Divine Providence even in the face of exile, genocide, and assimilation. Against all rules of history and sociology, this tenacious faith has allowed us to pass these tests and preserve us as a people. We've been bruised and battered, but we're still here, handing down

---

∗ **The Heroism and Martyrdom of Chanah and Her Seven Sons:**
At the time of the Maccabees, the Greeks tried to humiliate the Jews and tear them away from Judaism.

Chanah and her seven sons were brought before King Antiochus, who ordered each son to bow down to an idol of the king.

One by one, each of the brothers refused, citing their belief in the God of Israel. Each was brutally killed in front of Chanah. When it came to her youngest son, Antiochus promised him riches and honor if he would agree to bow down. But he too refused. The king offered mercy to the son if Chanah would tell him to bow down to the statue.

Instead, Chanah kissed her son and said, "My son, listen carefully to my words: I carried you for nine months, nursed you for two years, and have fed and cared for you up to this very day. To the best of my ability, I have taught you about God and the Torah. Do not exchange your commitment and loyalty to Judaism for the fleeting offerings of a king who will soon perish himself... ."

With that, Chanah watched her seventh son go to his death. Standing by the bodies of her sons, Chanah prayed for the souls of her children, for the strength of the Jewish people, and to be taken by God rather than be killed by the Greeks. As she finished her prayer, she breathed her last breath and fell dead beside her children.

It is the loyalty and courage of great Jewish women like Chanah who have perpetuated our precious heritage and inspire us until today.

—*Adapted from Rabbi Shimon Apisdorf, "Chanah's 7 Sons," aish.com.*

our values and histories from generation to generation. We have kept faith in God's Providence, trusting God and accepting whatever He has placed upon us.

If we're faced with a test of faith, we are free to choose the outcome. Suffering may be thrust upon us against our will, but we choose how to face it. As I wrote earlier—but this is so critical that it bears repeating—adversity doesn't define us; how we respond to adversity does.

> *Herman Wouk, the novelist and author of This Is My God, offers a relevant analogy: These people [referring to the Jews who choose to assimilate] are lost to Judaism, that is all; lost down a road which has swallowed many more Jews than the Hitler terror ever did. Of course they survive as persons. But from the viewpoint of an army, it makes little difference whether a division is exterminated or disperses into the hills and shucks off its uniforms.*[24]

A soldier in wartime who strips off his uniform and goes AWOL may have saved his own skin, but he is lost to his fellow soldiers and to their overall mission. That AWOL soldier made his allegiance to himself, not to his platoon or to his mission. Sometimes the choice is stark— *bow to the cross or you will be killed*—but more often the challenge is internal, as we decide whether to trust God or to rail at the heavens. Or both!

In God's operating system, tests are a feature, not a bug

While I was in the hospital after my wife had been pronounced dead, I had a detailed conversation with myself.

Life as you have known it has changed forever. This is the opportunity to put all that you have learned and all that you believe in to the test, I told myself. *Am I up to it? Can I take it? Can I internalize what has until now been a theoretical idea? Can I live with that idea? Can I even embrace it?*

This was the biggest test I ever faced in my life: to accept God and not reject Him or speak against Him while suffering a monumental personal loss. It was a struggle, and I hope I lived up to it.

Judaism is not only about what you do, it's also, perhaps primarily, about *who you are.* After all, you can keep every commandment meticulously and still be a lout or a scoundrel. For example, you can check off all the boxes, pray by rote, eat only kosher food, observe the festivals, and otherwise be completely *observant,* but you could nevertheless be oblivious to the reasons *why* you're keeping the commandments, and Whose commandments they are. The purpose of the commandments is not only about the logistical details, such as not turning lights on and off on Shabbat or technical aspects of ritual, such as wearing a *tallit* during prayer. Those practices exist to help you create a framework for God-consciousness. If you keep these *mitzvot* with a God-consciousness, you will gain the gift of true, meaningful connection. If you do them only by rote, good for you for doing so, and you'll be checking off the boxes, but you'll be missing out on the soul connection that everyone craves.

Our tests are meant to raise our consciousness of God and bring us closer to Him. If we're fortunate, our tests will involve small setbacks and only moderately sad events, but we will be spared extreme or ultimate tests.

But many of us do face a tragic event: an ultimate test that shakes us to our core. That is when we must face ourselves and perform a real self-examination, taking stock of our strengths and weaknesses, and our assets and liabilities. Can we use this tragedy as a springboard to figure out how to best utilize our strengths and assets, and how to minimize our weaknesses and liabilities? Conducting this evaluation will teach us more about who we are now versus who we can still aspire to be. Moreover, we can also assess who we really are in relation to God, the architect of the tragedy.

Only we can decide whether to give this personal crisis the power to destroy us—or whether we will choose life and forge ahead in a positive direction.

It's certainly not easy, but I believe we have the strength to stand up to whatever test comes our way, to never buckle completely under our pain or grief. We can find it within ourselves to embrace God and say, "God, I don't understand what You're doing, but I know it comes from You, so I accept Your challenge wholeheartedly," or, "I accept it reluctantly," or, "I will have to struggle with it until I accept it."

Here's why this matters so much. If we see a test as a glitch in God's operating system, a system failure that caused an unpleasant or even tragic event to happen to us, then we become a victim. If, however, we recognize that tests are part of God's plan for our growth and development, and that they exist to make us stronger, then we are not victims. Instead, we are full participants in life.

In other words, in God's operating system, tests are a feature, not a bug!

Our ability to pass God's tests of faith depends on our attitude toward adversity. "We can discover our meaning in life by the attitude we take toward unavoidable suffering," wrote psychiatrist and Holocaust survivor Dr. Viktor Frankl. "Everything can be taken from a man but one thing: the last of the human freedoms—to choose one's attitude in any given set of circumstances, to choose one's own way."[25]

Chapter Summary: *Judaism teaches the belief that every aspect of our lives has purpose, which means that our suffering has meaning and purpose, as well. Some suffering is meant to refine our souls; other suffering can be seen as a test of faith in God. Because God is unknowable, we may never understand why He allowed suffering to visit us in the first place. Through developing our faith, we can understand and accept that there are reasons for God's actions that are beyond our vision and comprehension. This understanding and acceptance keeps us from feeling victimized by seemingly random occurrences. Ultimately, while we cannot choose what happens to us in life, we can always choose the response of faith and commitment, and we can choose to not let tragedy defeat us.*

Endnotes:

1   *Avot* 5:3.

2   Job 1:10–11.

3   Ibid. 2:7; 9–10.

4   Ibid. 2:11–13.

5   Ibid. 38:1–21.

6   Ibid. 39:26–29.

7   Ibid. 40:4–5.

8   *Bava Batra* 15a-b.

9   Genesis 22:1.

10   Ibid. 17:2.

11   Commenting on Genesis 22:16.

12   Psalms 11:5.

13   Chapter 3, discussing Midrash, *Bereishit Rabbah* 32:3.

14   Genesis 12:1.

15   Deuteronomy 6:5.

16   *Igrot Kodesh of the Sixth Lubavitcher Rebbe* (Brooklyn, NY: Kehot Publication Society, 1984), Vol. 8, letter #2193, November 15, 1943.

17   I Chronicles 28:9.

18   Genesis 32:29.

19   Devora Freund, "I Am Staying," *AmiLiving Magazine*, Issue #487, September 30, 2020 (12 Tishrei 5781).

20   German-American scholar, philosopher, and poet (1921–1980); a "self-described heretic," according to Dennis Prager in his *The Rational Bible: Exodus* (Washington, DC: Regnery Faith, 2018).

21   Dennis Prager, *Ultimate Issues* magazine, Vol. 4, #1, 1988.

22   Habakuk 2:4.

23   Psalms 91:15.

24   From *This Is My God* by Herman Wouk, copyright © 1987. Reprinted by permission of Little, Brown and Company, an imprint of Hachette Book Group, Inc.

25   Viktor E. Frankl, *Man's Search for Meaning* (New York: Washington Square Press, 1959).

CHAPTER EIGHT

The Holocaust

"Silence! Thus has arisen in the thought [of God]!"
—*Talmud, Menachot 29b*

It is with trepidation that I approach writing about God's role in the Holocaust. The magnitude of the event is so overwhelming that to reduce it to words is fraught with peril. It is difficult to encompass the enormity of the number six million, let alone what it means in the context of "The Six Million." If you look at the number written out—6,000,000—the mind almost shuts down. We have no way to even begin to absorb its meaning. About such matters that are so incomprehensible, the Talmudic instruction, "Your silence is better than your speaking,"[1] surely applies.

Having said that, if I'm writing a book about theodicy—understanding how we can say God is good when evil exists in the world—and I'm seeking to explain why good people suffer, the topic of the Holocaust cannot be avoided.

I am neither a philosopher nor a theologian. I'm just a regular Jew, born after the Holocaust, trying to serve

God, live responsibly, and make sense of life. What I offer is one man's way of coming to terms with what no one can really come to terms with.

The Holocaust presents a challenge to make sense of both life and death. Understandably, the vastness of its murderous depravity has turned many people off from God entirely.

I recognize that minds far greater than mine have struggled with and written about the Holocaust for two generations. Their opinions span the gamut from postulating that God Himself, as it were, was murdered with the six million (as odious and blasphemous as these words are to the ears of a believer) to that the Holocaust was punishment for any of a thousand sins or wrongdoings.

In attempting to find meaning in the Holocaust, the writer is in a no-win situation. Finding an answer—as if this were even possible—in effect rationalizes and therefore "justifies" the event. This is just too inconceivable to countenance. This would also be a desecration of the memory of the six million murdered, and perhaps also a desecration of God Himself.

Some have said that the Holocaust was "necessary" because the State of Israel became a reality as a result. In making this association, they offer a "reason" for the Holocaust. Now, if one had asked a Zionist in 1940, "Would you barter six million Jewish lives for getting a state?"—no moral person would have agreed to that deal. There can be no hypothetical scenario of any "cost-benefit" analysis presented *before the fact* of the Holocaust that could ever justify its *actualization*. An explanation *after the fact* does not make it legitimate unless it would have been justified *before the fact*. I do not believe that any moral human being can come to terms with this. Likewise, any other beneficial result given for the Holocaust would have to pass the same test, and each would fail.

An alternative viewpoint that some have argued is that the Holocaust has no meaning; it's a theological black hole in Jewish history. Such a thought, floated by so-called theologians and other thinkers, goes contrary to the abiding principle of Judaism that God plays an integral role in human events, especially events surrounding His Eternal People. And as for the six million victims,* can we dare

---

* Dispute concerning statistics on the number of Holocaust victims does not only come from deniers of the Holocaust:

An oft-cited statistic of five million non-Jewish Holocaust deaths has no basis in fact, experts say, and may be contributing to [Holocaust] denial efforts.

This number was contrived by Simon Wiesenthal, a Jewish-Austrian Holocaust survivor, Nazi-hunter, and writer who died in 2005. Holocaust historian Yehuda Bauer said he warned his friend Simon Wiesenthal about spreading the false notion that the Holocaust claimed eleven million victims—six million Jews and five million non-Jews—but that Wiesenthal replied, "Sometimes you need to do that to get the results for things you think are essential."

Wiesenthal had told Bauer and other Holocaust historians that he chose the five million number carefully: He wanted a number large enough to attract the attention of non-Jews who might not otherwise care about Jewish suffering, but not larger than the actual number of Jews who were murdered in the Holocaust—six million. The number five million also adheres to no known understanding of the number of non-Jews killed by the Nazis. While as many as thirty-five million people were killed overall because of Nazi aggression, the number of non-Jews who died in the concentration camps is no more than half a million, Bauer said.

Deborah Lipstadt, a professor of Holocaust studies at Emory University in Atlanta, wrote in 2011 how the number continues to dog her efforts to teach about the Holocaust.

"I have been to many Yom Hashoah, Holocaust Day observances—in-

172 WHY GOD WHY?

say that their cruel deaths have no redeeming meaning? Finally, if God has nothing to say about the Holocaust, does He not forfeit His credibility in all other matters?

So, paraphrasing the Talmud,[2] "Woe is to me if I speak, woe is to me if I don't speak."

The ostensible "death of God" is greatly exaggerated

The claim that God also "died" during the Holocaust is, to borrow a quip from Mark Twain (on the topic of Twain's rumored demise), "greatly exaggerated."

The God of the Bible and of the Ten Commandments did not die in the crematoria.

In fact, if any loss of faith arises from the Holocaust, it should be a loss of faith in any human-based morality. In nineteenth-century Europe, the German people epitomized an enlightened culture and scientific advancement. They were known for their polite manners, organization, appreciation of art and music, and philosophical morality. The ethos that accompanied that culture proclaimed they no longer needed the God of the Bible, and that they

cluding those sponsored by synagogues and Jewish communities—where eleven candles were lit," she wrote in an article in the *Jewish Review of Books* in which she lacerated Wiesenthal's ethical standards. "When I tell the organizers that they are engaged in historical revisionism, their reactions range from skepticism to outrage. Strangers have taken me to task in angry letters for focusing 'only' on Jewish deaths and ignoring the five million others. When I explain that this number is simply inaccurate, in fact made up, they become even more convinced of my ethnocentrism and inability to feel the pain of anyone but my own people."

—Adapted from Ron Kampeas, "'Remember the 11 Million'? Why an Inflated Victims Tally Irks Holocaust Historians," *The Times of Israel*, February 1, 2017

were capable of establishing and supporting their morality with their own superior societal norms.

German philosopher Friedrich Nietzsche, a self-proclaimed nihilist, made the famous (or infamous) statement, "God is dead" (*Gott ist tot*), because, in his view, the Enlightenment had proven the triumph of scientific rationality over sacred revelation. Appropriately enough, one of Nietzsche's books was a collection of essays titled *Beyond Good and Evil.* In those writings and in others, he railed against organized Western religion and the tendency of religion to shun worldly pleasures and delights. He said that no one needed to rely on the crutch of old-time religion and God when we had achieved such heights of technological and philosophical achievement.

These very same "enlightened" and "cultured" people devised and perpetrated the most vile atrocities known in human history. This should rightly put the final nail in the coffin of the gods of reason and science and the gods of atheism—yes, atheism is a religion, too.

Without loyalty to the One God, all rules governing society are subject to moral relativism

The same goes for the "enlightened" Western powers who slept* while the six million were murdered. The Western nations outside Germany bankrupted their moral authority by permitting the Holocaust to continue and by condemning to death hundreds of thousands, if not millions,

---

* Arthur D. Morse, *While Six Million Died: A Chronicle of American Apathy* (New York, NY: Random House, 1968)

whom they refused to admit as refugees in their lands. The United States' own record is shameful, having denied asylum to hundreds of thousands[3] of desperate European Jews. More than nine hundred asylum seekers on the German ocean liner *St. Louis*, nearly all Jewish, were turned away from the port of Miami and sent back to Europe, where more than a quarter died in the Holocaust.

German barbarism and the cold neglect among so many Western nations about the plight of the refugees taught us a lesson for all time: *A moral and civilized existence cannot be based on or maintained by "enlightened" human beings who cherry-pick their morality and ethics.* A moral and civilized existence is possible only through belief in and acceptance of Divine authority. That's why the moral dictates of *You shall not steal,*[4] *You shall not murder,*[5] and *You shall not covet*[6] are in the Ten Commandments, right there alongside *I am the Lord, your God,* and *You shall not have other gods besides Me.*[7] By the way, these "other gods" certainly include the gods of enlightenment, reason, science, and culture.

Without loyalty to the One God, all other rules governing society are subject to moral relativism or human whim.

So why *did* the Holocaust happen? This brings us to the suggested explanation that it was punishment from God for His people's sins. During the Holocaust, many pointed to the irreligiosity of assimilated European Jewry as such "sins." They based this claim on parallels in the Torah and the books of the Prophets.

The analogy doesn't hold true, however, because the

prophets, including Moses, Isaiah, and Jeremiah, *were channeling God and speaking on His behalf.* They prophesied that impending disastrous events, including the destruction of the First and Second Temples in Jerusalem, *would* be punishment for sin. They were conveying that which they heard prophetically from God. This gives their statements an authenticity that is lacking in related statements made by commentators, philosophers, or even rabbis voicing their personal opinions or interpretations. God did not speak to any human being in this manner during the twentieth century, neither before nor after the Holocaust. And rabbis, no matter how wise and pious, are not prophets.

In a public talk, the Lubavitcher Rebbe, Rabbi Menachem Mendel Schneerson, most emphatically rejects the idea that the Holocaust was a punishment for sins of the generation that experienced it:

> The destruction of six million Jews in such a horrific manner that surpassed the cruelty of all previous generations could not possibly be a punishment for sins. Even the Satan could not possibly find a sufficient number of sins that would warrant such a genocide. There is absolutely no rational explanation for the Holocaust except that it was a Divine decree; why it happened is beyond human comprehension.[8]

The Rebbe rejected *all* theological explanations for the Holocaust. What greater conceit—the Rebbe would say—and what greater heartlessness can there be than to give a "reason" for the death and torture of millions of innocent men, women, and children? We can only concede that there are things that lie beyond humanity's finite

understanding. The Rebbe was echoing his saintly fa-
ther-in-law, the Previous Lubavitcher Rebbe, Rabbi Yosef
Yitzchak Schneersohn, who would say: "It is not our task
to justify God on this. Only God Himself can answer for
what He allowed to happen."

Another daring and controversial approach was articulated most eloquently by the late Rabbi Dr. Norman
Lamm, a renowned Torah scholar, rabbi, author, and former chancellor of Yeshiva University. Focusing on the
concept of *hester panim,* "the hiding of God's face," Dr.
Lamm wrote:

> During an extended period of historical national hester
> panim, *which would be from after the destruction of the
> Second Temple in 70 CE to the* Shoah (Holocaust), *we
> are given over to the uncertainties of nature and history,
> where we can be raised by the tides of time and cir-
> cumstances to the crest of the world's waves—or hurled
> pitilessly into the fierce troughs of life. Neither our suc-
> cess nor our failure means anything during this stage of
> hester panim... . Such was the period of the Holocaust.
> It was the ultimate expression of meaninglessness, and
> that was, perhaps, the ultimate blow to its victims... .*
>
> *This is, I confess, a bold assertion: that other than
> God's role in preserving us, there is no clear "sense"
> or "meaning" in Jewish history since the destruction
> of the Second Temple. I agree that this is a worrisome
> proposition. But our sacred sources not only support
> this, they point to it. We are in a state of* keri, *of hapless
> aimlessness. We are, as the Sages put it in the Talmud,
> "excommunicated by heaven."*[9]

God may be hidden, but He is never absent

With my utmost respect for Dr. Lamm, I cannot abide this approach. The Jewish concept of God is that of a *personal and supervisory* God, even during times of *hester panim,* as we recite often, *Behold, the Guardian of Israel neither slumbers nor sleeps.*[10] The Sages of the Talmud[11] spoke of the *silence* of God as a historical fact, but not of His *absence.* In contrast, Dr. Lamm describes a people *abandoned* by their God. Someone who is described as *hiding his face* is still able to observe and supervise the one being watched, though the one who is being watched may feel alone.

In our thrice-daily *Amidah* prayer, we acknowledge "God's daily miracles for us." Daily miracles? What? Where? When? The Talmud says, "Even the one to whom the miracle occurs doesn't recognize the miracle."[12] That is not abandonment; that is God providing miracles when He so chooses, behind the scenes.

In the Book of Esther, we read the story of Purim, when Persian Jewry was saved from a genocidal decree by Haman, the chief adviser to King Ahasuerus. The die seemed to have been cast and the Jews' fate sealed. But an eleventh-hour turnabout sealed Haman's fate as an insidious evildoer, and the Jews' terror turned to *gladness and light.* Nowhere in the entire drama is God's behind-the-scenes role revealed. In fact, the name of the heroine of the event, Queen Esther, is interpreted in the Talmud as related to the very same concept of *hester panim.* For over two thousand years, Jews have celebrated God's Providence on Purim and been reminded that while we may not always see God's countenance or obvious actions, He is always an active director in the unfolding of history.

The agnostic's serendipity is the believer's Divine Providence.

The term that Dr. Lamm uses, *keri,* or "hapless aimlessness," is from the Torah,[13] and Maimonides discusses this concept in his *Guide to the Perplexed.* But with all due respect to Dr. Lamm, *keri* cannot be reconciled with the established concept of Divine Providence.

This leaves us with the logical if still troubling conclusion that if everything is by Divine Providence, the Omnipotent God was surely aware of and consented to the Holocaust. Can we live with such a conclusion?

Shall the Judge of the earth not do justice?

In pre-Holocaust Jewish history, Jews met with unjust suffering through the most terrible persecutions and genocidal attempts at the hands of countless oppressors. These include the eleventh-century Crusades; chronic expulsions from European cities and towns throughout the Middle Ages and early modern ages from England, France, Spain, and other lands; Passover blood libels; pogroms; economic and social anti-Semitism—the sad list goes on and on. The great British historian Paul Johnson considered anti-Semitism a singularly "peculiar" category of racism, calling it an "intellectual disease, a disease of the mind, extremely infectious and massively destructive."[14] No wonder that millions of Europeans so willingly became swept up in the Nazi agenda. The dehumanization of Jews among so many societies over the millennia prepared the ground for Europe's general acceptance of the Holocaust.

Given this history, Maimonides instructs that we warn any prospective convert, "Why did you choose to convert? Don't you know that the Jews are afflicted, crushed, sub-jugated, and strained, and are befallen with suffering?"[15]

The Holocaust would not have shaken the faith of the believing Jews of 1940 who read aloud from the *Hagga-dah* at the Passover Seder, "In each generation they rise over us to destroy us." They knew about the destruction of the two Temples, the Crusades, and the pogroms, and yet they kept their faith. This same foundational belief in God was employed by many during and after the Holocaust.

Devastating anti-Semitic persecution was nothing new. The Holocaust was novel only in its magnitude, systematic cruelty, technological advancement, and the warped "master race" anti-Semitic cynicism that drove it.

The philosophical question, "Shall the Judge of the earth not do justice?" applies *qualitatively* to the seeming-ly meaningless suffering of a single individual as much as to that of six million individuals. Obviously, the suffering of one or a few can be more easily explained by one of the theodicies—one of the explanations of how we can say God is good when evil exists in the world—which cannot be done for the Holocaust.

The Talmud states, *"Din pruta k'din mei'ah*—the judg-ment of a dispute regarding a *pruta*, a minuscule mone-tary sum, is to be dealt with identically as the monetary judgement of one hundred *maneh* (pounds of silver) [or ten thousand dinars—one million, nine hundred twenty

thousand times as much]!"[16] When dispensing justice, the quantity in dispute has no bearing on the quality of the justice that must be dispensed. Likewise, even one instance of unjustified suffering or a tragic death is equivalent to the injustice of six million deaths. In fact, to the individual who experiences a tragedy, it *is* a personal Holocaust.*
Now, if we presume that a just God is duty-bound to intervene and impose justice regarding each individual and in each circumstance, as it *might* be expected of Him, we need to return to the suggested theodicies that allow us to come to terms with such issues.

But no theodicy would apply to the Holocaust, the tragedy of tragedies.

We now understand that not all human suffering re-

---

* The Jewish radical theologians of our day, such as Dr. Richard Rubenstein—author of *After Auschwitz*: *Radical Theology and Contemporary Judaism*, 1966, and a leading voice in the "death of God" movement—also challenged the notion of a cosmos-controlling God. He and numerous less-degreed people—whose preoccupation with the problem of the Holocaust led them to the conclusion that the Holocaust had invalidated the idea of an omnipotent, benevolent deity—failed to understand the true nature of the quandary of faith after the Holocaust. The problem of faith here is a problem of theology in the broadest sense of the word. What becomes questionable is the manner in which God relates to the world and to man. As far as one's faith in a personal God is concerned, there is no difference between six million, one million, or the hundreds of thousands murdered in historical pogroms.

Nachmanides expressed this thought clearly in his *Shaar Hagemul* (*The Gate of Reward*). See: Nachmanides, *Writings and Discourses*, Vol. II (Brooklyn, NY: Shilo Publishing House, Inc. 1978): "Our quest [regarding theodicy] is a specific one, about [the plight of] this [hypothetical] particular man.... This problem is not reduced if those who fall are few in number; nor does it become more serious if their numbers increase. For we are not discussing [the ways of] man.... Our arguments concern *The Rock, Whose work is perfect and all His ways just; there is nothing perverse or crooked in them* (Deuteronomy 32:4)."

flects punishment or *any* of the theodicies. For example, the first suffering of the Jewish people on a massive scale occurred during the exile to Egypt and our enslavement there. This Egyptian exile was preordained when Abraham had his first encounter with God, during which they entered into a covenant called *Brit Bein Habetarim*, the Covenant Between the Halves.[17] This was decreed when Abraham was seventy years old, thirty years before his son Isaac was born. God told Abraham that his future progeny would be exiled and oppressed in Egypt for four hundred years. At the time, there were no Jewish people to talk about, just a promise that there would be a nation—one with a tragic future. If it was destiny, it obviously could not also be a punishment. The only insight we have into this is the Bible's term for the Egyptian exile—an *iron crucible*,[18] meaning that the bitter experience had a purpose.

Job has become the archetype of the innocent sufferer. When God finally speaks to Job, He doesn't offer him a simple answer for his travails, such as, "Satan threw down the gauntlet, and I picked it up. You were, unfortunately, the innocent victim!" Rather, to the extent that there is *any* answer in God's closing soliloquy, it is simply that God reiterates His transcendence to Job.

The Talmud says that Moses had been shown that the great teacher Rabbi Akiva would suffer a tortuous death at the hands of the brutal Romans. When Moses saw that they were weighing Rabbi Akiva's flesh in a butcher's meat market, he exclaimed, "Master of the universe! Is this Torah and is this its reward?!" The answer that came from Above was, "Silence! Thus has arisen in the thought (of God)!"[19]

This leaves us with the dilemma that in addition to the Holocaust, we have three additional instances where the answer to unjust suffering appears to be no answer at all:

1.   Abraham's prophetic "promise" of exile.
2.   God's non-response to Job for his suffering.
3.   God's non-response to Moses for Rabbi Akiva's cruel and tortured death.

With this as background, let me introduce you to God, the Unknowable One. That's not the God the *Unknown*. It is God the *Unknowable One—*He *can't* be known.

In earlier chapters we discussed the various theodicies (punishment, test, refinement, etc.) as possible explanations for our suffering. We looked to these theodicies in an attempt to find the meaning in suffering, to see which fits. But if all these fail, the ultimate theodicy is that suffering comes from God, the Unknowable One.

Doctor, put down that scalpel, now!

To make this idea relatable, imagine a primitive man who time-travels from the past to a modern operating room to witness open-heart surgery. The observer watches in horror as the surgeon makes the incision. Lacking any knowledge of modern medicine, the man concludes that what he is witnessing is murder in cold blood. He protests vigorously at this assault on justice.

Try and explain to him that the operation he is about

to witness is, in fact, a life-saving operation. With this explanation, this primitive man might come to understand that the procedure is purposeful and beneficial. The gap between what he knows and what the surgeon knows is one that cannot be bridged at all.

Relative to God, we are all primitives in His operating room. From our narrow, human perspective, we might impugn the surgeon, unable to see that the operation was purposeful and meaningful.* Yet from God's unfathomable perspective, that operation might be the most crucial, fundamental event in history.

Here we come to an important concept first alluded to earlier—the two manifestations of God: the Transcendent and the Immanent. *God the Transcendent* refers to God as He is by and for Himself—unrestricted, infinite, and inherently indescribable. But as we have discovered, God wants to have a relationship with His human creations. Therefore, He harnessed, restricted, contracted, and even contorted Himself into a persona to Whom we can relate. This is *God the Immanent* (literally: "existing or operating within"), Who fits himself "within" His creation, so to speak. This makes Him present in every detail of the world and in our lives. This is how He chooses to make Himself relatable.

---

* I state *purposeful and meaningful* but specifically omit using the word *beneficial*. In the analogy of the operation, we can appreciate the *benefit* of the lifesaving procedure. In the analogue it is *only* the transcendental purposefulness that we can talk about, not what the unfathomable *benefit*, if any, might be. We should not want to ascribe benefit, because that draws us back to ascribing a reason that we can appreciate, and it doesn't exist other than as a matter of trust and faith in God. *This distinction cannot be overemphasized.*

All the theodicies that allow us to explain God's plan for us are from the Relatable, Immanent God, Whom we are meant to understand—to the extent that we can. That aspect of God has to justify Himself to us, as it were. But God the Transcendent does not have to justify Himself. In fact, He cannot do so. No man or woman can understand such a God, not even the most highly developed and sophisticated among us. God's essence and His presence are entirely beyond our grasp.

Try this simple exercise: Can you imagine a state of being that is beyond time and space? We cannot comprehend what that means, yet the world of physics acknowledges that some scientific theories strongly suggest that there is existence beyond time and space. In other words, things exist that we simply are incapable of comprehending.

We have little trouble accepting the idea that what we can experience through our senses is not all there is. We cannot comprehend anything that lies in the "field beyond the field," in the unknowable aspects of the universe. That's because we are limited to experiencing everything in our familiar framework of time and space. If there is a God, He is unlike any other being. He *always* existed, always. This means He existed before time was created, because He created Time itself. He exists *everywhere*, as He created the dimension of space and so transcends the limitations of space as we know it.

This God Who preceded and created everything that we know is necessarily unknowable to us. This is axiomatic, a basic, elementary truth.

Once we have met the Unknowable God, we can appreciate that there is *no* satisfactory answer to why there was a Holocaust. The question is unanswerable. It is unknowable because it *lies beyond the limits of human experience or understanding*. Indeed, concerning this matter, Torah commentators, most notably the Shaloh, conclude[20] that the essence of knowledge is to know that we cannot know. Seven hundred years later, Ralph Waldo Emerson came to a similar conclusion, saying, "Knowledge is knowing that we cannot know." These were pretty wise people.

As thinking human beings, we yearn to understand things, but we should be careful not to fall into the trap of expecting to understand everything. As writer H. L. Mencken satirically observed, "There is always an easy solution to every human problem—neat, plausible, and wrong!"[21]

A leading twentieth-century philosopher, theologian, and Talmudic scholar named Dr. Eliezer Berkovits framed our conundrum this way: "All the ingenuity spent on the solution of the problem of the theodicy will not convince us that evil is not real, that undeserved suffering is so only in appearance, that life does not abound in irrationality and meaningless destruction."[22] The only way to frame this is by recognizing that the imponderable comes from the Unknowable One.

God did create men and women in His image, but that doesn't make us into little gods. Rather, we must approach the Creator with humility, as He says:

> For My thoughts are not your thoughts, nor are your ways My ways, says the Lord.

186 WHY GOD WHY?

> For as the heavens are higher than the earth, so are My
> ways higher than your ways, and My thoughts than
> your thoughts.[23]

The very exercise of trying to figure out how we can justify the Holocaust is itself problematic. When we ask *"Why?"* we are really asking how we can possibly understand and accept that God allowed this to happen. The question itself is inoperative, because we can't ever "understand" the "mind" of God!

"I know the answer, but I cannot tell you."

In quantum physics, it is impossible to know both the precise position and velocity of a particle. The reason has nothing to do with instruments that aren't yet sophisticated enough to take the measurements. The problem is that measuring the position and velocity of the particle requires hitting it with light. When you hit the particle with light, you affect both its momentum and position, which means you no longer know what the momentum and position originally were. This is known as Heisenberg's[24] Uncertainty Principle—*to observe something is to change it.*

Essentially, when we try to measure the position and velocity of the particle, we interact with the system, therefore affecting and changing the particle itself. We can never pretend we are fully objective outside observers. The act of trying to know something impacts the things that we are trying to know.

Now imagine the following scenario: Someone asks a seven-year-old child, "Tell me, what is the precise velocity and location of a particular particle?" The child would answer, "I don't know." If you had asked brilliant physicist Stephen Hawking the same question, his answer would have been, "I don't know." While neither of them knew the answer, there is a world of difference between the child's "I don't know" and Stephen Hawking's "I don't know." Stephen Hawking knew *why* he couldn't know. He understood that, based on everything we know about science, it is *impossible* to know. The answer to the question cannot be known.

The renowned author, lecturer, and counselor Rabbi Manis Friedman recounted to me that Elie Wiesel was often asked why God had allowed the Holocaust. His usual answer was, "I don't know."

At one lecture a young person was pestering him with the question excessively. Finally, Wiesel said to him, "I know the answer, but I cannot tell you."

"Why not?" he shouted.

Wiesel answered, "Because if I answer you, you'll become a Nazi!"

What did he mean? Wiesel was saying that if one can propose an answer for the Holocaust, if the Holocaust could be rationalized, we would have crossed the line separating humanity from Nazi-like thinking and behavior. The Nazis held that the Holocaust was justified. If we could find a rational explanation, if we can even entertain a justifiable reason, how would our core humanity be different from that of a Nazi?

Why we really don't want to understand the purpose of suffering

We can drive ourselves crazy trying to know or understand what we cannot possibly know. But there is another hidden cost to seeking to understand the mystery of why innocent people suffer. If we were to know the mind of God and see the ultimate purpose in the suffering, we would risk becoming comfortable with monumental tragedy. We might lose our moral judgment and clarity by implying that we could reconcile ourselves with suffering, even on the mind-boggling scale of the Holocaust.

We must keep boundaries between our intellect and delving into certain concepts, because the very effort can be corrupting. This means that trying to justify God's actions can lead us to take refuge in morally questionable rationalizations. One day, When Mashiach comes, God will allow us to understand the reasons why, and then our objections to suffering and evil will no longer be relevant. We will no longer be burdened by trying to understand or rationalize the Holocaust from our earthly, human perspective. For now, God is withholding the answer.

God is never AWOL. There is—however hidden from us—purpose and meaning in our pain and suffering. Sometimes, we do later see the answer to our question of "Why?" There are instances in which something clearly good comes from an unfortunate incident.

For example, I remember when a strapping young man in his twenties walked an elderly rabbi to his home in an unsafe neighborhood. As they approached the rabbi's house, they were accosted by hoodlums. The rabbi's protector fought off the hoodlums, but in the scuffle, he suffered a concussion. The rabbi insisted that he be examined in an emergency room. There, the young man was given an MRI and kept overnight for observation. The radiologist found a brain tumor, which was removed shortly thereafter. This unfortunate altercation experience, complete with a body injury, turned out to be a lifesaving gift!

Even while, unlike the story above, we generally have no answer that we are able to integrate and come to terms with, we have a surprising benefit from our incomprehension: We become outraged and energized to do everything in our power to prevent further evil from ever happening again. Perhaps this is exactly what God wants.

When Moses first encounters God at the burning bush, God intends to appoint him to lead the Jewish people out of Egypt. Moses was a shepherd, pasturing sheep in the Midian desert, and he was suddenly riveted by the sight of a burning thorn bush that miraculously continued to burn without being consumed. Moses says, *Let me turn aside and see this great sight: Why will this bush not burn itself out?*[25]

Then God calls out to Moses from the bush and says, *Do not come close; remove your shoes, because the place on which you are walking is holy. I am the God of your forefathers, Abraham, Isaac, and Jacob.*[26]

How did Moses respond to this extraordinary event? We're told, *Moses hid his face, because he was afraid to look at God.*[27]

Jewish Bible commentators make much of this encounter. They interpret God's dramatic introduction of

Himself to Moses as a burning bush that would not be consumed as symbolic of the idea that *God is with him [the one suffering] in his distress*,[28] meaning the suffering of the Jews throughout history,[29] even in the Holocaust's crematoria. God wanted Moses to understand the purpose of suffering ... from *God's* point of view. But Moses hid his face because he didn't want the answer. Why not?

Moses intuited that if he were to look at God's face, as it were, he would see the truth of God's justice. Moses' refusal to "look" and understand God's ways was in conflict with God's mission for Moses to become a leader of the Jewish people. Moses was saying, in effect, "If you want me to be the leader of Your people, I *must* not and *will* not possess any understanding that explains their suffering. I must be there to defend them totally, without any reservations whatsoever. If You empower me to understand Your justice, I will fail in my mission to be the faithful shepherd of Your people."

Like all of us, Moses *initially* wished to understand suffering. But when it came to the moment where God would reveal the answer, Moses backed away. He dared not understand God's inner workings at the cost of losing his humanity. Moses chose closeness with his flock over that with his Master. That is what sealed Moses' role as a true leader of his people.

How do we become God's partners in creation?

The 2004 Indian Ocean earthquake and tsunami took the lives of roughly two hundred twenty-five thousand people. Rabbi Lord Jonathan Sacks reacted in this manner:

The religious question is not "Why did this happen?"
but "What then shall we do?" The religious response is
not to seek to understand and thereby accept. We are
not God. Instead, we are the people He has called on to
be his "partners in the work of creation."[30]

Taking this idea deeper, the only adequate religious response to suffering on a grand scale is to say, "God, I do not know why this terrifying disaster has happened, but I do know what You want of us: to help the afflicted, comfort the bereaved, send healing to the injured, and aid those who have lost their loved ones, livelihoods, and homes."

Since it is fruitless to look for an answer to suffering, we must instead search for ways to make it end.

As we now understand, if this ultimate question about why the innocent suffer were answered, we would be able to make peace with the suffering of innocents. We would no longer be bothered by their cries or feel their pain, because we would understand why it is happening. And that is unthinkable.

Imagine that you are in a hospital, and you hear a woman groaning and moaning with pain. Outside her room her family is standing around chatting, all smiling and happy. You berate them: "What's wrong with you? Can't you hear how much pain she is in?" They answer, "This is the maternity ward. She is having a baby. We are happy."

When you have an explanation that great good will come from someone's pain, the pain doesn't seem so bad

192 WHY GOD WHY?

anymore. We can tolerate suffering when we know why it is happening—that it is the precursor to something wonderful.

If we could make sense of innocent people suffering, if we could rationalize tragedy, then we could live with it. We would be able to hear the cry of children in pain and not be horrified. We would tolerate seeing broken hearts and shattered lives because we would have neat explanations.

But as long as the pain of innocents remains a burning question, we will be animated to try to find a way to heal it. As long as we can't explain pain, we are driven to try to alleviate it. As long as the suffering of innocent people conflicts with our values, we will work to eradicate it.

We probably cannot stop ourselves from continuing to ask the question, "Why do bad things happen to good people?" even though we now understand that this question is unanswerable because God is unknowable. Instead of looking for answers, we need to take our righteous anger and turn it into a force for good. Channel your frustration with injustice into a drive to fight it. Combat the pain in the world with goodness. Alleviate suffering wherever you can.

God chose to keep quiet about His reasons for permitting suffering, perhaps to compel us to help each other.

He is waiting for us. That's what we are here for.

Chapter Summary: The Holocaust presents an enormous challenge to making sense of both life and death. For many, it also presents a challenge to serving God. Examining various theodicies to find possible explanations for this massive and unprecedented evil still leads us back to ground zero: the impossibility of finding any satisfying answer. God is unknowable. Even if we could understand His reasons for creating suffering, we might not want to know, because once we see the bigger picture and the ultimate reasons for pain and suffering, we would become desensitized to the suffering of others. What God wants instead is for us to channel our outrage and sympathy to do acts of goodness and kindness, and to bring healing and justice wherever we can.

Endnotes:

1   *Gittin* 4:8.

2   *Keilim* 17:16.

3   For statistics on the United States' frequent failure to save many refugees from Nazi Germany while the war was still going on, see the Constitutional Rights Foundation's lesson, "United States Asylum Policy": https://www.crf-usa.org/bill-of-rights-in-action/bria-10-2-a-united-states-immigration-policy-and-hitler-s-holocaust.

4   Exodus 20:13; Deuteronomy 5:17.

5   Ibid. (*both* sources mentioned in endnote 4 above).

6   Exodus 20:14; Deuteronomy 5:18.

7   Exodus 20:2–3; Deuteronomy 5:6–7.

8   *Sefer Hasichot* 5751 (1991) (Brooklyn, NY: Kehot Publication Society, 1992), Vol. 1 (*Parshat Vayechi*).

9   Norman Lamm, "The Face of God: Thoughts on the Holocaust," in B. H. Rosenberg and F. S. Heuman (eds.), *Theological and Halakhic Reflections on the Holocaust* (New York, NY: Rabbinical Council of America, 1992).

10   Psalms 121:4.

11   *Gittin* 56b.

12   *Niddah* 31a.

13   Leviticus 26:24; 28.

14   Paul Johnson, "The Anti-Semitic Disease," *Commentary*, June, 2005.

15   *Mishneh Torah,* Laws of Prohibited Relationships 14:1.

16   *Sanhedrin* 8a.

17   Genesis 15:13.

18   Deuteronomy 4:20.

19   *Menachot* 29b.

20   Rabbi Yedaiah Penini Bedarshi, *Bechinot Olam* 8:2, as discussed by Rabbi Yeshayahu Halevi Horowitz (*Shaloh*), *Shenei Luchot Habrit* 191:2.

21   H. L. Mencken, *Prejudices: Second Series* (New York: Borzoi Books, Alfred A. Knopf Publishers, 1920).

22   Eliezer Berkovits, *God, Man and History* (Jerusalem: Shalem Press, 2004).

23   Isaiah 55:8–9.

24   The German physicist Werner Heisenberg stated this principle in 1927.

25   Exodus 3:3.

26   Ibid. 5–6.

27   Ibid.

28   Psalms 91:15.

29   Rabbi *Naftali Zvi Yehudah Berlin* (the Netziv, 1816–1893), *Haamek Davar*, Exodus 3:3.

30   Rabbi Lord Jonathan Sacks, "Why Does God Allow Terrible Things to Happen to His People?" *The Times of London*, January 1, 2005.

CHAPTER NINE

The Afterlife:
Heaven, Hell, and Seeing the Light

Rabbi Yaakov says: "One moment of bliss in the Afterlife is more beautiful than all the life of this world."

—*Avot 4:17*

I knew a young woman—I'll call her Miriam—who suffered from an incurable congenital condition that ultimately took her life. Miriam was wise and very determined, and despite all her suffering, she managed to maintain a cheery and even spunky demeanor. At twenty-five she married a wonderful and loving husband. Between her periodic stays at the hospital, she often said, "It is going to be good at the end, and if it's not good, it's not the end." She died at twenty-nine.

I was struck by the profundity of Miriam's statement and her far-reaching insight into what it meant to reach "the end" of her physical, earthly life. After all that we have carefully explored on the weighty subject of theodicy, how can we still not feel a sense of injustice about Miriam's life ending at only twenty-nine? To paraphrase Moses' charge before God: "Master of the universe, why is it that the righteous suffer?"[1] Jeremiah offered a classic corollary complaint: *Why does the way of the wicked prosper?*[2]

Surely both Moses and Jeremiah knew the things that we have explored so far in this book about the unknowable aspect of God. Surely, both understood why these questions are unanswerable—at least in this earthly life. But if even *they* cried out with these questions, certainly we cannot help but also cry out with the exact same question: Where is God's justice? Will there ever be a time when all will actually be good at the end, a time not only when our pain and suffering will have ceased, but when we will be able to see in retrospect that it had all been just?

This brings us to a discussion about the Afterlife, where our soul ascends after passing from this life. This is the time and place when life's unfinished business gets worked out and when all *will* be good. This is the World to Come we've been waiting for. It's the world that Miriam anticipated—a world of clarity and ultimate spiritual contentment.

The inverted moral universe of the Afterlife

But, you may say, come on! Do you really believe in an Afterlife, that you and I will live on as souls after we die? How do you know? As the classic cynical quip goes, "Has anyone come back from there to report on it?"

The answers are yes and yes! Yes, I believe that this will happen to you and to me. I believe that the soul lives on, and this is not an outrageous, unrealistic, anti-science, or extreme position. It is true and consistent with sound scientific theory. And yes, someone did come back and report on his experience there.

The Talmud[3] tells of Rabbi Yosef, the son of Rabbi Yehoshua ben Levi, who fell ill and slipped into a comatose state (some commentaries are of the opinion that Rabbi Yosef had died, momentarily). When he was subsequently revived (or came back from his near-death experience),* his father asked him, "What did you see

---

* My knowledge of and belief in the Talmud makes it a reliable source to me, even for matters that stretch credulity, though I realize that some may remain unconvinced. If so, let's talk about the "near-death experience" (NDE) phenomenon:

There are many documented stories of those who were clinically dead—no breathing, no heartbeat, no brain activity—from a traumatic accident or who died on the operating table and were later resuscitated, and they recount what they experienced. Initially, I was skeptical about this, but the countless reports are too well documented, often by respected and unbiased scientists, many of whom were initially quite skeptical themselves. I submit that there must be something to it.

Near-death experience (NDE) reports share many common elements worldwide, indicating that they originate in phenomena independent of culture. Some of those who have had NDEs are young children with few preconceptions about religion or the Afterlife. Many of these individuals—adults as well as children—were aware of what was going on around their clinically dead bodies. They experienced themselves hovering above the scene, observing the car crash or the operating theater. They saw their entire life's events scrolling before them. Many describe traveling through a tunnel with a pinpoint of light at its end, emerging in a world that many describe as being filled with light, beauty, pleasure, joy, and unconditional love. Many tell of being greeted by long-dead relatives.

Traditional scientists cast doubt on the veracity of these experiences, understandably, as science deals with observable and verifiable phenomena. Some neuroscientists hypothesize that an NDE is a subjective phenomenon resulting from "disturbed bodily multisensory integration" that occurs during life-threatening events. Though they have no experiential proof of this hypothesis, it is what is proposed. Others have said that many scientists typically have a bias against professed spiritual phenomena. Yet there are other scientific researchers, originally skeptics themselves, who

over there?" He said, "I saw an inverted world! Those up-permost (in this world) are below (in the Afterlife), and those lowly (in this world) are above (in the Afterlife)." To which his father replied, "My son, you have seen an accurate (picture of the) world."

It requires open-mindedness to be willing to read about this subject and even to write about it. This is be-cause we are trying to understand abstract and ethereal dimensions of existence that we cannot imagine. In this chapter, I will delve into the most pertinent among these abstract and ethereal ideas to help us understand the Af-terlife and its purpose. More specifically, I will explore the following topics:

1.   **What is a soul?** Can we describe it? Can we under-stand its role and function in our lives?

2.   **One's body dies; one's soul does not.** While the body is buried in the earth, the soul ascends to a spiritual plane of existence. There, it experiences a cleansing process in preparation for the ultimate reward and delight of being in God's presence.

3.   **The Afterlife is where the soul goes after this life.** This is the address where all the apparent loose ends, unfinished business, and moral injus-

---

have been convinced by the preponderance of evidence that it is more than "disturbed bodily multisensory integration," and is in fact a portal into an-other dimension of existence.

I am not trying to certify the authenticity of the NDE literature. I'm sim-ply suggesting that for some, secular sources may bolster interest in and un-derstanding of the phenomenon of the soul living on after the body's death.

tices of this life are resolved. Heaven and hell* are part of the Afterlife.

4. **The soul remains aware of its earlier life.** The soul retains consciousness of its previous worldly life. It also transitions through stages of realization and refinement, leading to the ultimate enlightenment. By working through these stages, the soul finally sees that which was there all along, hidden in plain sight. This insight, or "heavenly light," gives the soul a new retrospective awareness concerning what took place during its worldly lifetime.

The descriptions of what takes place in heaven and hell are metaphors for matters of another dimension. "The righteous sit with their crowns on their heads and luxuriate in the radiance of the Divine Presence."[4] This is a reference to heaven. References to the "fires in *Gehinnom*"[5]—the Hebrew word used for hell—are metaphors for hell.

Judaism's metaphors do not include devils with pitchforks shoveling souls into a hellish inferno, nor of martyrs consorting with seventy-two virgins in heaven. The name refers to the valley [*gai*, meaning valley] belonging to a person called Hinnom (or Hinnom's Valley), located to the southwest of the Old City of Jerusalem. There, in the days of the prophet Jeremiah, some Jews worshiped the idol Molech by leading their children through fire and

---

* Hell is a Christian concept and is associated with eternal damnation. The Jewish idea of *Gehinnom* is more correctly termed "purgatory," which denotes purging and cleansing, after which the soul continues on to heaven and Divine bliss. For smoother readability, I use the word hell while meaning purgatory.

sacrificing them to the idol! Jeremiah warned the Jews, *Behold: Days are coming [as punishment for this cruel and dastardly idol worship] when this place will no longer be called the valley of Hinnom, but the Valley of the Killing. In this place I shall void the counsel of Judah and Jerusalem, and I shall make them fall by the sword before their enemies, and I shall lay out their carcasses as food for the birds of the heavens and the animals of the land.*[6] The Sages found a perfectly apt metaphor for a hellish setting in this valley of Hinnom.

In Jewish literature there are metaphors that reference two types of hell: One runs hot and the other runs cold. The *Gehinnom* of fire is for sins of anger, passion, and generally sins of *commission*. In contrast, the *Gehinnom* of snow is designated for sins of *omission,* such as slothfulness, apathy, callousness toward others, or being "cold" to one's obligations. We can all appreciate the metaphorical and figurative symmetry of these sins to their punishments.

What is a soul, anyway?

To reach a meaningful understanding of what a soul really is, let's start at the beginning. The Torah describes the creation of Adam (mankind: gender-neutral) as: *God formed man out of soil from the earth, and He blew into his nostrils a soul of life; and man became a living being.*[7] Unlike the rest of the creatures, which were fashioned as integrated living beings, the human being is unique—the only being created as *two* separate entities: body and soul. Adam's body was an inanimate, earthen clod until God "blew" his soul into him, infusing him with life. Blowing requires strength and energy, and through this "blowing," God transferred part of His spirit into Adam. This is why we believe that within every person there is a spark of the Divine.

Ask people to describe a soul, and you'll get many different definitions; the subject is obscure and esoteric. We all stretch to find a definition. I suggest that before we can describe the soul, we first need to be able to define *ourselves*. Who and what are we? Are we our bodies or our souls?

If we ask ourselves, "Who am I?" we intuitively sense that we are not exclusively our bodies, limited by our physicality. We also have feelings, emotions, and intellect, which are also not physical. When I refer to "my body," I am conscious that there is an *I* who inhabits the body.

Well, then, does that mean that I am defined by my mind (intellect) and my feelings (emotions)? Since I can and do change my mind and feelings, which are transient, moving targets, my mind and feelings cannot be who I truly am. Perhaps, then, is the *I* the conglomerate of *all* my parts—the physical as well as the intellectual and emotional? If so, then I am a hybrid with no essential, unifying core. And if that is, indeed, the case, who and what am *I*?

The Jewish approach to these questions is that the moving parts of our consciousness—our mind and our feelings—are like garments in which we wrap ourselves. We can easily see how this is true regarding our personas, the changing identities we display to the world and by which we invite others to perceive us. For example, if you're in middle management, you're someone's supervisor, and you have a superior over you. You adapt your persona for each role accordingly. We inhabit many personas, depending on the occasion. We alter our personas as easily as we change our clothes from office attire to workout clothes for the gym.

Returning to our question: Who am I? I posit that *I* am my consciousness, which I define as *the universal sense of myself that inhabits my being.* My consciousness houses my mind and feelings and acts through them, selectively choosing what elements of myself to display in my personas. This *I* is our core. It is a manifestation of our soul.

> *Rabbi Schneur Zalman of Liadi, known as the Alter Rebbe, held his young grandson, little Menachem Mendel, later the third Lubavitcher Rebbe, known as the Tzemach Tzedek,* in his lap. [Speaking Yiddish] the child called out, "Zeide, Zeide! [Grandfather, Grandfather!]"*

> *The Alter Rebbe asked him: "Where is Zeide?" The grandson pointed to his grandfather's head. The Alter Rebbe said, "This is the head, not Zeide." The child then pointed to the Alter Rebbe's heart and said, "This is Zeide." The Alter Rebbe replied, "This is the heart, but*

---

* **Rabbi Menachem Mendel of Lubavitch** (*Tzemach Tzedek*) 1789–1866: Chasidic rebbe and noted author. The Tzemach Tzedek was the third leader of the Chabad Chasidic movement and a noted authority on Jewish law. His numerous works include halachic responsa, Chasidic discourses, and Kabbalistic writings. Active in the communal affairs of Russian Jewry, he worked to alleviate the plight of the cantonists, Jewish children kidnapped to serve in the Czar's army. He passed away in Lubavitch, leaving seven sons and two daughters.

not Zeide." The grandson continued to point to the other parts of the Alter Rebbe's body in order to find the place where "Zeide" was. To all these attempts, the Alter Rebbe replied that he had indicated a specific limb of Zeide, but not Zeide.

The child climbed down from his grandfather's lap and began walking around on his own. When he approached the door, he pretended that his fingers had gotten caught in the door and began to yell, "Zeide, Zeide!"

The Alter Rebbe turned to the child and said: "What is it, my child; what happened?"

The child replied: "This is Zeide!"[8]

The soul is our life force and our purpose

In the book of Job, we read that the soul is *a part of God above.*[9] I'll stick with this definition. Alternate terminology for the same concept is a "ray of God" or a "spark of God." Mystical Judaism describes the soul as an ethereal, Godly energy that channels God's purpose for each of us. It acts as our life force.

As a life force, our Godly soul—the ethereal, spiritual core—animates the body. The body provides a physical home for the soul. *Our soul's manifestation in our body is seamless, harmonious, and intimate.* As long as our souls remain within our bodies, we are alive and do not experience disparity or apparent conflict between the body and soul elements. Only when the soul leaves are the two elements separated. As the verse states, *When his spirit departs, he returns to his earth.*[10] The person and his soul are no longer with us.

Those who have been present at the bedside when a loved one passes may be profoundly struck by the question, "Where did the person go?" Those who are not as spiritually inclined might simply say, "He's gone!" Period. Full stop. They might also argue that the recently departed life force had never been a spiritual soul in the first place.

Judaism takes a different view. Unlike the expression that pronounced President Abraham Lincoln's death, "Now he belongs to the ages," the Torah describes a man who has died as having been *gathered unto his people*.[11]

The soul didn't die. It just moved to another stage and state of existence, reunited with those who came before.

If there is a God Who is *the* Creator, He created and creates everything: the universe, the dimensions of time and space, and all that is in them. He creates each grain of sand, each blade of grass, every animal, and every human being. He didn't create them capriciously, but for a purpose. Let us call that Divine creative force "the soul" of each entity, which gives it both its existence and its purpose.

The Previous Lubavitcher Rebbe, Rabbi Yosef Yitzchak Schneersohn, related the following incident regarding the soul and how it reflects the purpose of each creature:

> It was the summer of 1896, and my father (Rabbi Shalom DovBer Schneersohn,* the fifth Lubavitcher Rebbe)

---

* **Rabbi Shalom DovBer Schneersohn (Rashab), 1860–1920:** Chasidic rebbe. Rabbi Shalom DovBer became the fifth leader of the Chabad movement upon the passing of his father, Rabbi Shmuel Schneersohn. He established the Lubavitch network of *yeshivot* called Tomchei Temimim.

and I* were strolling in the fields of Balivka, a hamlet
near Lubavitch. Walking and talking, we entered the
forest. Engrossed in what I had heard, I absentmindedly
tore a leaf off a passing tree. Holding it a while in my
hands, I continued my thoughtful pacing, occasional-
ly tearing small pieces of leaf and casting them to the
winds.

"The holy Ari," (a fifteenth-century mystic), my father
said to me, "says that every leaf was created by the
Almighty and is imbued with a Divine life force, created
for a specific purpose within God's intent in creation.
How can one be so callous toward a creation of God? It
has a body, and it has its life. [True, as a human being,
your purpose is different and superior to that of a leaf.
But the leaf was inherently fulfilling its purpose, which
you have disrupted.] In what way is the 'I' of this leaf [in
its class] inferior to yours [in your class]?"[12]

No, I cannot tell you the purpose of a specific leaf or
blade of grass, or of our neighboring star Alpha Centauri
or of the Crab Nebula. I have no need to know it; I only
need to know that it was created by God, and, as such, it
serves a purpose in His Godly plan.

When the body dies, where is the soul?

In trying to find an answer to this question about where
the soul goes when the body dies, I used a phrase earlier:
"ascends to a spiritual plane of existence." That is admit-
tedly very abstract.

He authored many volumes of Chasidic discourses and is renowned for his
lucid and thorough explanations of Kabbalistic concepts.

* He was sixteen years old at the time.

In trying to understand this, let's ask what happened to the theorem $E=mc^2$ when Albert Einstein died. Did his theorem die with him? And where was that theorem before Einstein advanced it? The obvious answer is that it existed before Einstein and continues to exist after him. It is an intellectual concept that exists on a different plane, in the dimension of the mind. Einstein was the first to articulate it, to draw it down so that it could be understood, debated, tested, and proven. We can try to transpose this framework of the existence, plane, and consciousness of Einstein's theorem to the soul in the world of the Afterlife.

No form of matter or energy is ever "lost" or destroyed

Furthermore, the Lubavitcher Rebbe, Rabbi Menachem Mendel Schneerson, would often point out that the principle of Conservation of Matter—a basic law of physics known as the First Law of Thermodynamics—is that no energy or matter is ever "lost" or destroyed; it only assumes another form. If this is true regarding physical matter or energy, how much more so regarding a spiritual entity such as the soul? The soul's existence is not bound by time, space, or any other delineators of the physical state. The spiritual energy that infuses the human being—and is the source of sight, hearing, emotion, intellect, will, and consciousness—does not cease to exist merely because the physical body ceases to function. Rather, it passes from one form of existence—physical life as expressed through the body—to a higher, exclusively spiritual form of existence.

Birth transitions are not only for newborns

The soul's transition when it leaves the body and ascends to continue its spiritual life can be compared to birth. A developing fetus in the womb is cocooned in protective and temperature-controlled amniotic fluid, nurtured and nourished organically by its mother. It is astonishing to realize that the environment that is required for life within the womb is not just dramatically different, but completely opposite to the environment necessary for life after birth. Specifically, for example, the immersion in amniotic fluid that keeps a fetus alive *in utero* would drown a newborn infant, who requires air to breathe.

When labor ends, the fetus is thrust into a radically different world, no longer floating in nourishing amniotic fluid but exposed to air, light, noise, temperature changes, much greater physical space, and human touch. This is our first transition from one form of life into another. Given the shockingly opposite environment a newborn baby experiences in her first moments of life, can you blame her for wailing?

After our "birth transition," our lives as physical human beings commence.

Likewise, the transition of our souls to the Afterlife reflects dramatically different worlds. For those who identify their *I* solely as their bodies and accoutrements, when they die, they—their bodies, et al.—will deteriorate, be buried, and—as far as they are concerned—be no more. But for those who identify their *I* as their souls, when their bodies die, they anticipate that their souls will begin the ascent to life everlasting. Judaism believes that the soul has an eternal existence. After death, it is no longer tied down by the body's physical needs and desires or by the limitations of our worldly intellectual and psychological vision of what life is all about. Like shedding a raincoat on a sunny day, the soul is free to rise to new heights, to its original, spiritual reality.

During our lifetime we also "die" many times, figuratively speaking, only to be reborn dramatically different and better. Like the caterpillar that metamorphosed into a butterfly, we shuck off the "dead" husk of earlier personas to reveal a deeper core that was there all along, waiting to emerge from its cocoon. Ask yourself: Are you the same person you were when you were a child? Of course not. You are an evolved and improved person with maturity and wisdom, capable of perceiving yourself and the world around you with different eyes. A person in recovery who has earned years of sobriety is a transformed person from the addict of long ago. Such a person even marks a new birthday to commemorate this new life. *A baal* or *baalat teshuvah*—a man or woman, respectively, who has returned to Torah-observant Judaism—is not the same person they were before their awakening to a deeper spiritual potential.

Our bodies die, but our souls live on. We will be reborn into a new world with an enhanced and elevated type of perception.

We are all musicians in God's symphony

As we explored earlier, each individual soul is an expression of God's intention and vision for the life of that person. In this way, we might say that the soul expresses the *why* of the person's existence: its Godly meaning and purpose.

It isn't easy to access our soul's mission. That's because our soul is housed in a physical body that has endless demands for food, warmth, touch, sleep, and other comforts. It seems that the body is the albatross that never stops challenging and blocking the soul's—and God's—lofty purpose. What are we to make of this challenge?

Let's take the analogy of a musical composition. In this example, we might say that the soul of the composition is the composer's spiritual vision. The actual musical notes are the body of that vison. The notes, or body, actualize and express the soul within them. When God is the composer, His vision and purpose for us is the soul. Our body and human consciousness are the notes, carrying out God's vision for it during our lifetime.

The composer might have thousands of compositions swirling in his creative mind, but only when he structures his compositions with musical notes that are played on physical instruments will they bring musical joy to the audience. God wants us to be part of the music—by making the world's stage a better place than it was before we entered it from stage left, and before we exit, stage right.

The way that we actualize this purpose is by refining our animalistic natures. This is our Godly purpose.

The relationship among these three entities—the soul, the human body, and our consciousness—can be complicated and even muddled. Think of it in the way an actor relates to the character she portrays. While a good actor needs to identify as her character, she is not her character. She has a real life outside of the movie set. There is only one real person who is the actor.

Just as an actor would invite chaos into her life if she were to confuse her true self with the character she plays, our soul's sojourn into the body is similarly perilous, because the soul can become so swallowed up by its worldly character. For example: The body instinctively wants to eat so it can live, but that body does not instinctively know the purpose of its life. A body where the soul is predominant would eat to live; a body dominated by its physicality lives to eat. A person, complete with its soul, is more than a mere animal with a higher IQ. The soul is instinctively selfless, while the human psyche, influenced so heavily by physical and ego needs, is instinctively self-centered. Without finding that transcendent purpose, it can forget who it is and why it's on the world stage.

This is a deep concept. Our body houses our soul and our character. But our earthly deeds are what define and reflect our characters. Our actions in every sphere of our lives create a permanent record in the spiritual cosmos.

Thanks for finally turning on the music!

Why is there such confusion or even distortion between our characters and bodies, on the one hand, and our souls, on the other hand? We are bombarded in our earthly lives by contradictory or unhealthful messages, images, and selfish yearnings. They vie for our attention in an endless, confusing loop, pulling us away from what is most real, tricking us into thinking that something is urgent when it is meaningless, luring us away from what we know in our bones is fundamentally important. In other words, the reality we experience in this earthly life is inherently subjective, blurring the clear vision we would ideally have about life and its priorities.

For example, we're trying to save for a down payment on a house, but ... wow, look at that shiny new car on the lot: it's practically calling my name! My kid is trying to talk to me now, but let me check to see who just texted... I know I said I would schedule this time every morning for ten minutes of prayer or meditation, but I'm tired. I'm going back to sleep. These challenges are persistent, and the balancing act is constant.

When our souls ascend to heaven, we will no longer have to struggle trying to distinguish between objective and subjective reality. In the Afterlife, we will be completely liberated from this cacophony of mixed messages—the temptations of the material, physical, and even intellectual offerings. In the Afterlife, we will clearly see the one absolute, objective reality and truth of God and Godliness.

Let's stick with our music analogy a bit longer. Imagine that you had spent a lifetime, say eighty years, watching an orchestra perform a symphony on a screen—with the sound turned off. You had seen the conductor gesticulating wildly and the musicians using precise hand and arm movements to skillfully play their instruments. Still, you heard nothing: only silence. You might have asked yourself at times: Why are the people on the screen making all these strange, yet coordinated motions? What is the point? We may have had a vague notion that something wonderful was happening on that stage—that a great piece of music was being played—but we got used to the silence. After a while, the silence became normal. We didn't even miss hearing the notes!

In heaven we will watch that performance again, but this time with the sound turned on.

We are the members of the orchestra. Throughout each individual's lifetime, we are the musicians in God's symphony. Are we playing our instruments in a manner that is true to the Divine Composer's musical score? Or are we just trying to follow the zig-zagging notes of the scores of the latest trendy composers, whose work will be forgotten in a generation? During our lifetime we usually don't get feedback about the quality of our music-making. In the Afterlife, when the sound is on, the music we hear will reflect how we lived, the values we held, and the deeds we performed. Will it be melodious and graceful, or jarring and discordant?

The world of the Afterlife is the ultimate experience in values clarification

Earlier we referred to the Talmud's poetic allusion to life in heaven: "The righteous sit with their crowns on their heads and luxuriate in the radiance of the Divine Presence." We can now appreciate how our expanded consciousness in the Afterlife will enable us to perceive Godliness, and, along with it, truth, goodness, generosity, and enlightenment. This will become our new and clear perception of reality. This explains why, in many religious traditions, the death of a person who lived a righteous life is a celebration of a life well lived. The soul has achieved its goal and has now moved on—graduated, as it were—to a higher existence.

We imagine heaven and hell as places: heaven is the place where we hope to arrive, hell is a prospect too terrifying to consider. But, in reality, we make our own heaven and hell, and it's entirely based on how we live now. For those righteous people who managed, despite all of life's distractions and temptations, to play from the Divine Score, gaining this new perception of reality as being Godly may prompt them to say, "This is heaven!" For those who lived selfish, immoral, or evil lives, this new perception might prompt them to shout, "This is hell!"

The world of the Afterlife is the ultimate experience in values clarification. Reward and punishment in heaven might mean that we finally, ultimately realize what life was meant to be. Our souls will either take pleasure in having lived a life that validated these values or suffer from realizing how much of life we squandered pointlessly—or worse.

In the Afterlife we get to reflect on our worldly, painful struggles in retrospect. We will experience a paradigm shift—the confirmation that all our challenges were opportunities for refinement in preparation for this ultimate stage. The trials and difficulties we complained about, asking, "Why are these bad things happening to me?" are now rephrased as, "I now see that these challenging events happened for me."

This is what it means to "see the light." It can only happen once we enter the Godly realm, ready to receive our soul's Godly revelations directly.

The Talmud[13] contrasts the pain experienced by the souls transitioning from this worldly life to the heavenly life. For the righteous who merit dying by experiencing God's "kiss,"[14] their souls experience dying as painless "as pulling a hair from milk." For those at the other extreme, their souls' pain of death is "as a thorn entangled in wool fleece, which when pulled out backward rips out tufts of the wool." For the righteous, their souls' new environment poses no threat. It is a seamless continuation of their past, fulfilling the realization of all of their life's beliefs and aspirations. For those who wasted their lives, seeing the truth of what could have been will cause deep pain for their souls. The material acquisitions and conquests that we had defined as success during our earthly lives will, in the Afterlife, be understood as hindrances to *true life-affirming achievements*. When we finally experience God's truth, the shame of such a realization is devastating. One might call that hell.

Few people are all good or all bad, and we will all need a transition to the Afterlife. Think of that transition as a grand therapy session, in which layers of poor character and behaviors are painfully exposed and "cleansed" to make the soul's consciousness pristine and holy again, as it was before it descended into this earthly life.

Sometimes, this transition begins before death. For the person lying on his deathbed, and perhaps facing the people who have meant the most to them, the meaning and purpose of their life is often crystallized for them in those final moments. They may already begin to regret lost opportunities to connect to God, to family, and to friends; to strengthen the bonds of love, caring, and friendship as much as they worked to strengthen their financial portfolio. Their material achievements begin to pale in importance when compared to their most vital relationships. The familiar phrase, "Nobody on their deathbed has ever said, 'I wish I had spent more time at the office,'" is true!

My father's good death

My father, may he rest in peace, lived a good life. Oh, he worked very hard physically (he owned a printing company) and endured his share of tragedies. He came to the US with his wife and three children at the age of thirty-three, without a marketable trade or profession or even English proficiency. He lived hand-to-mouth while raising a growing family (six children altogether), but we children never knew what we didn't have. Our father always lived modestly. But more importantly: he lived a "good" life. By this I mean that he lived to do good. He was meticulously honest, a true role model for his children; he prayed three times a day to the very last days of his life, he learned Torah and taught it for as long as his stamina held out, and he was kind and caring.

The scene of my father's passing stands out vividly in my mind. Our longtime family physician who cared for him (in both senses of the word) informed us that his remaining time was short and the family should come together. My mother, all his children, and tens of his grandchildren and extended family were in his home that evening. Many were reciting Psalms. The doctor was there, too, and checked on him periodically.

Eventually, the doctor announced that the time was approaching. Our mother, all his children, and many of their children entered his room, surrounded his bed, and said the appropriate prayers for his soul as prescribed in our traditions. As it became clear that his soul was leaving his body, we all exclaimed in unison the Jewish creed, *Shema Yisrael* ... "Hear O Israel, the Lord is our God, the Lord is One," as he was "gathered unto his people."

His doctor later said that he had been present at many deaths, but he experienced this one as unique. He said, "It was as if his soul was carried aloft on a chariot of love!" My father died as he lived.

Chapter Summary: *God has created each of us purposefully, with a soul that lives within the body. As long as our souls remain within our bodies, we do not experience disparity or apparent conflict between the body and soul elements. Only when the soul leaves the body are the two elements separated. During our earthly lives, our perception about the meaning of our lives is clouded by earthly concerns. But when the body dies, the soul lives on in the Afterlife. This is where and when we will experience total clarity about life; we will gain, in retrospect, an understanding of all that happened to us, and why it was all for the good. How we live now determines whether seeing the ultimate truth will be heaven or hell.*

Endnotes:

1   *Brachot* 7a.
2   Jeremiah 12:1.
3   *Pesachim* 50a.
4   *Brachot* 16a.
5   Rabbi Eliyahu de Vidas, *Reishit Chochmah (The Beginning of Wisdom)*, *Shaar Hagemul (The Gate of Reward)*.
6   Jeremiah 19:6–7.
7   Genesis 2:7.
8   *Otzar Sippurei Chabad,* Vol. 17; adapted from the translation in Rabbi Dovid Shraga Polter, *Chassidic Soul Remedies: Inspirational Insights for Life's Daily Challenges* (Brooklyn, NY: Sichos in English, 2004).
9   Job 31:2.
10   Psalms 146:4.
11   Genesis 25:8.
12   *Likkutei Dibburim, An Anthology of Talks by Rabbi Yosef Yitzchak Schneersohn,* Vol. I (Brooklyn, NY: Kehot Publication Society, 1987).
13   *Brachot* 8a.
14   *Bava Batra* 17a.

CHAPTER TEN

What If There Is No Explanation? How Do We Reach a Place of Peace?

*There is not a single blade of grass that does not
have an angel in heaven that beats on it and says to
it, "Grow!"*
—Midrash, Bereishit Rabbah 10:6

At the beginning of this book, I explained that my purpose in writing it was to channel my experience of dealing with personal pain, based on the loss of my young wife many decades ago, into a comforting guide for others who have also been struck with tragedy. How can a good and just God allow such things to happen? Why, God? *Why?*

This is a timeless question—one that had been famously written about by another rabbi, Harold Kushner, in his 1981 book, *When Bad Things Happen to Good People*. I felt his conclusions not only failed to offer meaningful comfort to those suffering from the pain of loss, but that his conclusions were also inauthentic to Jewish belief. It was important to me to provide a broader and deeper dive into what Judaism has to say about this issue. I was impelled to do this not only for the sake of doing justice to God, but also to offer a framework that would be more psychologically and emotionally satisfying.

Losing Rochel Leah taught me many things. One of the

most unnerving among them was that the stock answers I had been offering from my rabbi's toolkit were inadequate when trying to comfort other bereaved individuals. My belief in God remained unshakable, but I realized that it was based more on the intellect than the heart. I felt that I could not afford to let God think I was angry at Him for taking my wife away from me and our eleven children. I did not want to show Him my deep disappointment.

I know that "the struggle is real"

I kept this disappointment and anger under wraps for years. With time, valuable therapy, and the wisdom and understanding of my new wife, Chana Rachel, I found a way to finally release my latent, lingering pain in a healthy way. I learned that allowing myself to feel—and even express—my anger at God did not threaten the relationship. In fact, I realized that the security I felt in my relationship with my Creator was precisely what allowed me to face those challenging emotions. All relationships have bumpy patches, including one's relationship with God.

It is not natural or easy for me to write so personally about my life. I am doing so only because I want you to know how deeply I know that the struggle is real. But the struggle can also be won.

In my situation, the key resolution was not in finally *expressing* my anger toward God. It was in acknowledging that I had been *suppressing* my anger at God, which manifested itself in the distancing, the cold shoulder, I had turned toward Him. The resolution was in recognizing how much I really needed my relationship with God. My self-indulgent nurturing of my hurt from my great loss, was counterproductive. So I chose to release myself and God from this grudge. I chose to accept God's decree, because I chose to accept that maintaining and strengthening my relationship with Him was much more important than nursing my grudge. This is what broke the logjam.

That is what worked for me. But every person is an individual, and what brought me freedom may not be the same as what you need. And so, in this, the final chapter, I want to briefly review the key Jewish approaches to why bad things happen to good people. These approaches—also called theodicies—attempt to reconcile how God can be both all-powerful and still good, even while allowing unfathomable pain and tragedy to afflict good people. I introduced these theodicies in Chapter 1.

Beyond that, though, I want to offer some additional ideas for those of you who have valiantly stayed with me so far and read all the chapters but are still unsettled and unsatisfied. You are still far from feeling the emotional freedom that I know is possible, a freedom from endless grief and anger at God.

First, a quick review of the theodicies—the explanations for unjust suffering under the auspices of a good and omnipotent God:

1. To refine one's character
2. As punishment for personal sins
3. As a test of faith
4. As afflictions of love
5. As related to a previous incarnation
6. As suffering that remains beyond a mortal's under-

standing but will be clarified and soothed in the Afterlife.

If your faith in God is absolute and God permeates the core of your being, you will more easily accept these theodicies, and that whatever happens in the world is God's will. But most of us aren't attuned that way. We try to fit events and circumstances into recognizable, predetermined, logical patterns to better understand what is happening. We try to fit God into these patterns, too, even though, by definition, God cannot be contained in any pattern devised by human beings.

However, as we have discussed frequently in this book—particularly in Chapters 5, 6, and 7—God does want us to understand and appreciate Him. He gave us moral and ethical frames of reference—our values—through the Torah, which are intended to inform our beliefs about how we should live our lives as individuals and as a society. These include God's definitions of justice, law and order, reward and punishment, and other big-ticket issues.

We see only what happened. We don't see God acting behind the scenes.

But as instrumental as these frames of reference are for many situations, they seem insufficient when we grapple with the painful, inexplicable things that happen to people. When an innocent person suffers a tragic circumstance, where, we ask, is justice? Why was a righteous person "rewarded" with an early death? When facing these questions, we are often at a loss.

A human being cannot know for sure why something

bad happens to another person or why God allowed it. We can only speculate, but even that is like shooting darts with a blindfold on. Consider how often we may be surprised to discover a deep truth about someone whom we have known for decades. Even that person's longtime psychotherapist may still not know with certainty why this person may have taken a surprising action that they didn't expect. If we can't know why our fellow mortals do what they do, how much more so are we unable to correctly guess why God has chosen to allow an unexpected, seemingly unfair thing to happen!

In earlier chapters we also discussed how we are especially bewildered and upset when a tragedy strikes a large number of people. We just cannot wrap our heads around the horror of hundreds of people dying when two jumbo jets collide, let alone hundreds of thousands of people perishing in a tsunami, or the millions who were murdered during the Holocaust. The numbers are so vast that they seem almost meaningless to us. They are not meaningless to God. We see only what happened; we don't see God acting behind the scenes.

Mission accomplished? How can that be?

When something bad happens to someone who, in our opinion, doesn't deserve it, it may be cold comfort to acknowledge God as the arbiter of that action. On the other hand, when a wicked person is sent to prison for decades, loses all his money, or ends up with a miserable life, we are probably okay with that. This aligns with God's ethical and moral frame of reference: *At least he got his just deserts,* we think with satisfaction. We still may not know exactly why things happened the way they did in his case, but we take heart in that "the Judge of all the earth" *did* justice.

But when something awful happens to a good person, we really don't know why. I knew a man aged sixty-two who stepped out of his car to deliver specially prepared matzah to a homebound individual for the Passover Seder. He got hit by a car as his wife and teenaged daughter watched. He died a day later. We're exponentially more upset by this case and, especially, in cases where the innocent person struck down is completely vulnerable—such as a child whose life ends through illness, accident, or, God forbid, violence. These situations wrench our hearts.

The man volunteering his time to deliver Passover matzah to a homebound person was purposefully doing a good deed. A toddler who dies of a sudden illness was a complete innocent. How are we to process these situations? The mystery nags at us: "Why this person?" Only God knows everything about someone's past and future.

In these cases, here is something to consider: Maybe God sent this good man's soul straight to heaven before he could do something wrong that only God could foresee. Maybe he had an old spiritual debt that remained in the Celestial Collections Department. The toddler's soul may have been sent down to complete an uncompleted mission from a previous life—I will share a story about this later in this chapter. Ultimately, only God can know the reasons why; we cannot.

Rochel Leah passed away from a genetic heart condition we were unaware of. Three months later, I read an article in the newspaper about what doctors had recently learned about that condition. Wow, I thought, if we had known this six months ago, my wife might still be alive. Then I responded to my own thought: *If we were supposed to know about her heart condition six months ago, we would have known about it six months ago.* If I had allowed myself to become fixated on this "What if?" situation, it would not have brought my wife back. God chose what information we had and when we had it. We can drive ourselves crazy by living in the past in this way. We need to live life by driving forward, which is impossible if we are constantly staring in the rear-view mirror.

Rochel Leah lived for thirty-six years. She accomplished a great deal during those years, not the least of which was bringing eleven children into this world and raising them with love and dedication for as long as she did. As we learned, the soul is eternal. For me, this provides the comfort of knowing that Rochel Leah, their mother, is aware of her children to this day from her heavenly perch. She is deriving *nachas*—prideful joy—from each of them. The question of why she died at thirty-six—and not at seventy-two or the proverbial one hundred twenty years—is not a question I can answer, nor one I can ask.

Apparently, her mission was fulfilled in thirty-six years, and when it ended, so did her life. I have to handle that for myself. So do my children—from the twins who were only sixteen months old and don't remember their mother, to the eldest child who was a teenager and took her death very hard. All of us, though, trust that God knew what He was doing.

It's impossible for human beings to accurately judge other human beings. So how can we judge God?

Hillel would say: Do not judge your fellow until you have stood in his place.[1] This makes it very clear that human beings are rarely in the position to judge other people. We may judge *actions*, but because we do not know the full background or context, we dare not judge another person. When a store clerk is rude, we don't know what miserable situation he is dealing with at home that has given him a short fuse that day. When we see a person we know to be wealthy only offering a small sum to a good cause we are collecting for, we cannot know what business reversals or catastrophic medical bills her family is facing.

We humans cannot judge, because we lack God's limitless insight. Can you judge a person whose life and values reflect her having grown up in a warm, wholesome, observant Jewish home as you would a person whose life and values reflect only secular influences with no consciousness of what Judaism is, or what God is, till the age of thirty? Only God can judge the flaws of these individuals, fully taking into account their backgrounds, though we speculate that God will be gracious to the person who grew up without Him.

Even a trained judge can judge only by what their eyes see and their ears hear. The judge can know a great deal of law and treat a rich person and a poor person equally, not favoring either one. But can they know what is deep in the heart of either person? If they judge by intangible criteria that they infer, and which encompass more than the facts of the case, the judge would be unfaithful to their oath to uphold the law. They would be acting more as a social worker or therapist than as a judge. If every court case were determined by the whim or personality of even the well-intentioned judge, it would make a mockery of God's admonition to judges, *Do not favor the judgment of a destitute person in his grievance.*[2]

And so, here is a fundamental question we must grapple with: If only God can know the true depth of every person's life before He passes judgment, how can we humans begin to conjecture about His actions, let alone judge them?

It is understandably axiomatic to Judaism that God always knows what He's doing. Our difficulty is that, on the one hand, God wants us to understand Him. On the other hand, the concept that God is unknowable doesn't help us understand Him to our satisfaction, nor does it help us find adequate explanations for the role He played in our suffering.

How do we know that God wants us to understand Him?

Why is God unknowable? It's not because He wants to distance Himself from us. It's not that He is unwilling to reveal Himself to the extent that we can handle such exposure. It certainly isn't because He has anything to hide. Although God is unknowable, we can get to know Him only within the boundaries of our limited human intelligence.

God is unknowable, by definition, because He is the Creator of heaven and earth.

If God is the Creator, He created not only the material aspects of earth and the ethereal aspects of heaven but also the dimensions of time and space in which heaven, earth, and all matter exist.

Think about it: If God created time, He must be outside and above it. If He created space, He must be outside of and beyond it. The same thinking applies to many abstract notions in our lives, such as knowledge, reason, judgment, and mercy. If God is the ultimate "meta"—if He is beyond all reason, knowledge, or emotion, by what metric can we expect to know Him?

God planned the world and the creatures in it for a purpose. Therefore, He ensures that we humans are created with the ability to relate to Him and to His purpose. He wants us to understand Him. How do we know? Because He revealed Himself at Mount Sinai and gave us His teachings. His teachings add a "because ..." to His instruction. At the revelation and in the Torah, God presented elements of Himself in the thought-form of a persona so that we would be able to relate to Him. The Midrash states that God appeared during the revelation at Mount Sinai as an elder filled with mercy. At the splitting of the Sea of Reeds, He appeared as a mighty warrior. And when God did speak, He spoke to the people *directly*: I *am the Lord,* your *God, Who has taken* you *out of the land of Egypt, from the house of bondage...* .[3]

Yet this direct communication from God to His people overwhelmed them; it was too intense—emotionally and spiritually overpowering. They feared that if God continued speaking to them in this revealed way, they would die.[4] That is why they asked Moses to relay the rest of the commandments.

Through the revelation and the Torah, we get to know God, His character, and His charter. The Torah is our ultimate guidebook for how we are meant to live our lives. He revealed Himself to us with this while still holding back: God did not, and could not, reveal *all* of Himself.

We can develop a personal relationship with God. Here's how.

There are many avenues through which we can develop a personal relationship with God: prayer, performing *mitzvot,* and trying to emulate Him in His aspect of giving and loving-kindness. When our relationship with God is personal, we relate and are related to. We appreciate and are appreciated. We can celebrate God or cry to Him—we know He's paying attention. Under certain circumstances we can disagree with God, saying, "We don't understand You. What You're doing seems inconsistent with the structure You Yourself set up for us and our relationship." We may even feel justified in challenging God. But when all the available answers and responses feel hollow or unsatisfactory to the inquisitive mind or pained heart, our only reasonable option is to accept the unknowable aspect of God. That means accepting His decrees while at the same time trying to remain open to feel His embrace.

Finding hope through history

Despite our pain, there are ways we can reconcile ourselves to suffering and find some kind of peace. Most of them involve purposefully shifting our focus from the here and now and instead gazing back into the past and forward into the future.

Let's take an example of a family who survived a natural disaster, such as a hurricane or a wildfire, but lost their home and all their possessions. They are in shock. Life as they had known it seems over forever. Then, as the shock wears off, they realize that many of their neighbors lost everything, too. Not only that, but they begin to realize that people have suffered similar disasters throughout history. When they view their catastrophe in a larger historical context, they find a bit of comfort and a glimmering of hope. They know that in the past people have rebuilt, and, therefore, they can rebuild, too.

Similarly, a person stricken with a debilitating ailment will almost surely discover that many others—thousands or perhaps even millions—have been through the same trials. You may benefit from being part of a support group with such people and learning some of their coping mechanisms.

If you lose someone close to you, you have memories to cherish and you can relate to their soul's continued presence, albeit on a higher plane, as discussed in Chapter 9.

No matter your circumstance, do not allow yourself to remain mired in grief. This cannot be overemphasized: You have a future to plan. Your loved one's soul will be pained, knowing that you continue to suffer.

Jews consider the soul to be immortal; it lives on after the body's death, in the Afterlife. The ultimate explanations we seek may not be available to us in this lifetime, as we explored in Chapter 9. Only in the Afterlife—when we have clarity of consciousness and our souls have been cleansed sufficiently so that we have earned the right to live in God's neighborhood, so to speak—will we understand. True, we are not entirely privy to what takes place there, but it is irrefutable that what we experience here on earth during our lifetimes isn't the full picture. What is unclear and confusing to us now may become clear in the next world.

Additionally, as we learned in Chapter 8, if we *did* understand our earthly suffering because we understand God's thinking and plan, we would lose our compassion and sense of pain at the suffering of others. We would lose our righteous indignation, our dedication to heal and offer comfort. That is too steep a price to pay. For now, we must trust that the soul understands what we're experiencing and so does God. When our souls enter the hereafter, we'll have a loftier and crystalline perspective on what took place while we lived in this world.

We are responsible to try to pass God's tests

In Chapter 7 we explored the idea that dealing with adversity is a test. Tests are meant to bring out our full potential. In that respect, they challenge us with "good stress." That's why it is so sad when someone who is tested by God and fails then faults God or someone else instead of taking responsibility for the failure.

I was once involved in a business deal that didn't work out, and I lost some money. I was angry at the other principals in the deal. Later, upon reflection, I realized that *I* hadn't done adequate due diligence. So I had to take responsibility for the part *I* had played in the arrangement falling through.

Anyone who has counseled a troubled couple or mediated a divorce knows that it's often futile to try to assess and assign which partner is wrong and by how much. It takes two to mess up a marriage, and it doesn't matter who was most to blame: each partner is tested. If there is any hope to repair the marriage, each person must own up to his or her share of the breakdown in the relationship. This takes courage, honesty, and maturity. But a much improved, deeper relationship is possible as a result.

Many of us in twenty-first-century America live relatively pampered lives. We have incomparably more, materially speaking, than our grandparents had two generations ago. Yet psychologically, we seem to be much poorer, with dramatically less resilience in coping with life's inevitable difficulties. When we are faced with a difficult or sad situation and want to draw on our inner resources, we may come up short.

People sometimes tell me, "I'm at the end of my rope. I'm about to have a nervous breakdown, and I can't find God anywhere." I know when they are being a bit overblown rhetorically, and I might take that statement with a grain of salt. I know they're hurting, I empathize with them, and I try to help them see the light at the end of the tunnel.

Often, though, they are denying their share of responsibility for their suffering. They are failing themselves. Contrast such people to the survivors of the Holocaust. Surely, they bore some trauma for life, but many developed near-superhuman psychological strength. Their survival instinct enabled them to shore up their resilience in a way they never dreamed possible. When adversity strikes, our job is to look deep inside ourselves, tap into our inner strength, and gird for the struggle ahead and the growth that can come from it.

Trauma can be transformative, opening a window into a new understanding of the self, and even a new understanding of how to live life. There is a name for this process: Post-Traumatic Growth Syndrome (PTGS). This is not simply resilience on steroids. PTGS refers to people who have had difficulty bouncing back from adversity in the past, but then—after experiencing a traumatic event that challenges their core beliefs—engage in a profound internal psychological struggle, ultimately emerging with significant personal growth that can affect almost every aspect of their lives.

People who have successfully experienced PTGS often report changes in the following five areas:[5]

1. Renewed or deeper appreciation for life
2. Ability to relate to others more personally and intimately
3. Discovering increased character strength and self-esteem
4. Exploring new possibilities and daring out-of-the-box thinking

5. Having a spiritual, existential, or philosophical
    awakening.

As people who have experienced PTGS have learned,
tragedy can also be an opportunity for spiritual refinement, our topic in Chapter 6. When you can see your travail as a door opening for new life lessons and personal
and spiritual growth, you will be in a better position to
heal, and even to reach a higher level of maturity. While
we would never choose this type of springboard to becoming better, stronger people, it is undeniable that applying this mindset can help us do just that. Notice people who have been through life-threatening or otherwise
dire situations but came through it: when they are inter-
viewed, or in the memoirs they write, they say consistently that they would not have changed the experience
for anything, despite the harrowing circumstances. They
emerge from these tests and afflictions reborn, with an
appreciation for life they never had before.

When "bad" becomes "good"

When we begin to see the broader perspective in our
lives, we realize that the bad thing that happened was, at
its core, intrinsically good because God, the Omnibenevolent, designed it to happen. Most of us lack the big picture,
so we must search for the good within the tragedy or misfortune. You will need to be patient and let enough time
pass until you can manage the situation calmly and begin
to reflect on it without allowing your sense of overwhelming emotion crush any other realizations.

Sometimes it doesn't take as long as we might expect. A

young woman I know fell down the stairs in her home and broke her foot. She and her husband had been scheduled to go on a two-week trip to the Caribbean a few days later. But with a broken foot and the woman immobilized, they weren't going anywhere. Because they were home and not in the Caribbean, her husband spent more time on LinkedIn, posting comments and contributing to discussions in his professional field. A higher-up in a healthcare company took notice of his comments and invited him to interview for a job. This young man had been dissatisfied at the job he then had at a poorly managed company and leaped at the opportunity. Two weeks and several interviews later, he had a far better job with substantially higher pay. The fall was then seen as a blessing. And yes, eventually they did go on their long-delayed vacation!

Do you remember the story I described in Chapter 1, of the young woman who became observant of Jewish tradition but a few short years later developed multiple sclerosis? She was angry—the disease trapped her in a deteriorating body and would eventually take her life. In fact, she died in her mid-twenties. At one of our last meetings, she shared with me, amid tears, that she had made peace with God, Whom she was going to meet in the not too distant future. She came to see the hell she was going through as a crucible in which her soul could reach a high level of purity.

I don't have a good answer to why she suffered so much and died so young. This I do know: Her soul lives on. Somehow, according to God's calculations, she had fulfilled her mission in this world and was deemed ready to go to the next one. I am confident that in the hereafter, her soul is enjoying a happy life.

"Your child had a greater mission than just being your son"

In that same chapter I shared another very tragic story of a doctor and his wife who lost their five-year-old child. They saw this tragedy as punishment for their no longer being sufficiently *shomrei mitzvot*—observers of the commandments. I assured the couple that God would not punish a child for his father's infractions. First of all, as I explained, each soul earns an accounting on its own merit, and a five-year-old's accounting is categorically different from an adult's, because the child is too young to be held responsible for his actions.

I told the grieving parents, "When you are ready, you need to focus less on the impact your son's death had on you and more on what his soul may accomplish in the future. Your child had a greater mission than just being your son. Only God knows what that mission is. Take comfort in the idea of reincarnation as understood in the Jewish mystical tradition, the Kabbalah: the concept that souls are 'recycled,' as it were, to complete their larger missions."

The following story may have been exactly what a couple bereft of a child needed to hear:

> *Once there was a couple who wanted a child but had been unable to conceive. The husband and wife went to the Baal Shem Tov and asked for a blessing that they would have a child, or at least for some advice. The Baal*

*Shem Tov was reluctant to give them such a blessing,
even though they asked for it many times.*

*Finally, the Baal Shem Tov surrendered to their pleas
and gave them the desired blessing. Within a year, the
wife gave birth to a healthy, robust, lovely, sweet baby
boy. The boy thrived until he was two years old, but just
before his second birthday, he suddenly died. The couple
ran back to the Baal Shem Tov and said, "What did we
do wrong? We did our best. We tried to be pious, good
people. We had a child, and now he is gone. Maybe it
would have been better if he had never been born."*

*The Baal Shem Tov said, "Let me tell you a story. A gen-
eration ago, there was a pogrom in a town not too far
from here. The Cossacks attacked the Jewish community, and in one house they killed an entire family, except
for a newborn baby. One of the Cossacks, who had no
children of his own, saw the baby in his cradle, and rather than kill him, the Cossack took the baby home and
raised him as his own.*

*"Two years later, the Cossack got so drunk that the po-
lice came to his house. They saw the child and realized
that he was Jewish. After they locked up the Cossack,
the police gave the child back to the Jewish community
to raise. The Jews found a foster home for the boy, and
he was raised as he was born, a Jew.*

*"The child grew up to be a good person, righteous and
pious. When his time came, and he stood before the
Heavenly Court, the judges said, 'He is a wonderful
person and deserves to go to heaven. But he has just one
blemish: For the first two years of his life, he was raised
in a crude Cossack environment, and that is a blemish
on the purity of this soul.' The Heavenly Court's deci-*

sion was to send the man's soul back to earth for two years, to redo the years he had lived with Cossacks and purify that blemished period."

The Baal Shem Tov said to the grieving couple, "You were not destined to have children. That's why, even after all your requests, I couldn't give you a blessing to conceive a child. But when this soul became available for a two-year adoption, I prayed for you, and you merited to give birth to and raise this child for two years. Instead of thinking you did something wrong and are being punished, be comforted that you had the merit of raising this soul for the two years that he needed in order to complete an unblemished life."

One of the Baal Shem Tov's basic teachings was that anything a person sees or hears bears a personal message—if it didn't, it wouldn't have been brought to the person's attention. When we are challenged by a tragic occurrence, we are obligated to try to figure out what its lesson may be. Sometimes you can figure it out for yourself, or you may need the help of someone whose wisdom and knowledge can help you reframe the situation better. There are numerous resources for such guidance. There are knowledgeable rabbis at Chabad Houses throughout the country and even internationally. The websites of Chabad.org and Aish.com are excellent resources where you can ask a rabbi anything through a pop-up message box.

You may never get to see the "why" of a tragedy, but there is always something you can learn from it.

The Previous Lubavitcher Rebbe, Rabbi Yosef Yitzchak Schneersohn, who led Chabad-Lubavitch through the

1940s, also played down the need for an explanation of tragedy, but with an interesting twist. Responding to the Holocaust, the Rebbe said:

> *You don't have the answer! I don't even have to hear what you say to know that you don't have the answer. Whether an answer exists or not, I don't know.*
>
> *But who says we have to find an answer to justify God? Let's let Him owe us one.*

If explanations for tragedy elude us, how can we move ahead with healing? How can we remove ourselves from the present and look toward the future with hope? How do we stop just going through the motions of life and reengage with the world?

Helping others is a pathway to healing and reengagement with life

After tragedy, it is all too easy to shrink into yourself and retreat from the world. But reengagement with life is essential, not only for you, but for your loved ones and the friends who care about you. Taking responsibility to try to pass this very difficult test is one way to reengage. Another is to see how we can be of help to others. We had several examples of this in Chapter 6, with people who started awareness and support campaigns about gun safety, drunk driving, infertility, and other important issues. When we are dedicated to living purposefully—a life not just lived but *examined*—we are fulfilling what God wants us to do and infusing each day of our lives with meaning.

We can't all start support or advocacy organizations, nor should we. But we can also reengage and live a deeper, more self-reflective, and future-oriented life by giving charity. In Hebrew the word for charity is *tzedakah*, which means "justice," revealing that in God's moral and ethical frame of reference, we are required to take care of others. If people are struggling to survive, it's our responsibility to help feed them, clothe them, and find them shelter. The Torah states, *If your brother becomes destitute and his hand falters beside you, you shall support him [whether] a convert or a resident, so that he can live with you.*[6] When people's basic needs are met, they will be more open to developing a value system that will allow them to examine their lives and make them meaningful.[7] Being involved in this effort is not only healing to others but is self-healing as well.

Friendships nourish our lives, and nurturing them is another effective way to look toward the future. *At all times love a friend; a brother will be born for adversity*, wrote King Solomon.[8] His message is that if you always have a friend with whom you can share news, arguments, and confidences, that friend will become as a brother— someone you can lean on when your heart is sore and your soul is troubled.

Yes, God is your Friend

In our splintered world, where family bonds have come undone in so many communities, the trick is to have such friends *before* you need them. If you haven't maintained the level of friendships where you can talk about serious topics and be fully yourself, you won't be able to suddenly snap your fingers and find one in a moment of crisis. You can't suddenly say, after a lifetime of closely guarding how much people know about you, "Who would like to be my friend? I need a friend right now!"

The Midrash identifies the "friend" mentioned by King Solomon as God.[9] He is the dependable, understanding companion we need. If you maintain a personal relationship with God during tranquil times and relate to Him frequently and with true feeling, that friendship will blossom into the loving support needed to sustain you through rough times.

Probably the best way to establish that relationship with God is through daily prayer. While prayer should ideally be an intense spiritual experience, it isn't always so for many. Perhaps not surprisingly, this can be especially true for those who pray daily, where routine can slip into rote. Your prayer experience may depend on whether you've had eight hours of sleep or four, or whether you've had your first cup of coffee yet. But *daven*ing (prayer, in Yiddish) is how you check in with God and keep up that conversation, even if sometimes your daily message to God is, "Nice talking with You, God, but I've gotta go to work now. See You later."

We also speak to God in the first person: We say, *"Baruch Atah Ado-noi,"*—Blessed are You, God. It is a one-on-One conversation. Also, Hebrew, the optimal language for prayer, is personal and intimate. It doesn't feel like "I and Thou"; it's me and You. And every once in a while, when you do experience a problem, a prayer in the *siddur* suddenly leaps out at you from the page with new, previously unrecognized significance. For example, if someone in your family becomes sick, you will find yourself saying

the daily prayer for healing with a previously unknown
intensity:

> Heal us, O Lord, and we will be healed; help us, and
> we will be saved, for You are our praise. Grant us a
> complete cure and healing to all our wounds, for You,
> Almighty King, are a faithful and merciful Healer.

Or if you have a big decision to make, perhaps the
prayer asking God for wisdom will resonate:

> You graciously bestow knowledge upon man and teach
> mortals understanding. Graciously bestow upon us Your
> wisdom, understanding, and knowledge.

The immediacy of prayer—along with its ability to
speak to us about our physical, emotional, intellectual,
and spiritual needs—fosters our feeling that God is vitally
and authentically our Friend. If you are mourning a close
relative, God forbid, and you need to be part of a *minyan*
quorum to say *Kaddish* (the prayer recited by mourners
acknowledging God's dominion), then you immediately
have a built-in support group to comfort you in your loss.
Two renowned authors have written books about what
the commitment to saying *Kaddish* did for them in terms
of having a built-in support group.[10]

Even good relationships can fall into a rut, and our relationship with God is no different. When things are going well, we can become smug and complacent. We may
take those closest to us in life for granted. With God, we
may relegate Him to the background, blocking Him from
having an active role in our lives. A crisis will change this.
Our smugness will be shattered, forcing us to reevaluate
our basic values. If we undertake this process with com-

mitment, we often find that our bond with God needs to be much deeper than it had been until then. We see a chance to renew the bond on a profoundly higher level.

During a crisis, you will need to draw on many sources of strength: prayer, time with friends, study, introspection, even arguing with God. Take the time necessary to deal with crisis. This advice is both practical and spiritually sustaining. Do you see what all these steps have in common? We must fight the all-too-human tendency to use tragedy and suffering as an excuse to push God away. By practicing these steps, we can bring God closer. This is what is called for in times of trouble.

The three driving forces of the human being and how they connect to dealing with crises

Our tradition sees the Jew as having two souls. One is a Divine soul that is inherently Godly: good and pure. This Divine soul is the stimulus for all the good, holy, and altruistic drives within that person. The counterpart to the Divine soul is an animal soul, which consists of the person's innate and instinctive desires that are generally self-centered, self-aggrandizing, and materialistic. These less lofty desires include the quest for creature comforts and fame. In most people, the animal soul is the active driving force.

There is yet a third force at work within a person. This is not a soul but an amoral, abstract, analytical, intellectual drive: the force within us that craves objective, untainted reasoning. Even before we introduce the concept of the Divine soul, this intellectual drive distinguishes us from animals. Because it is "amoral," it has no moral compass guiding it. This is why intelligent people can be so easily led astray by dangerous or foolish ideas. The ideas may have a certain intellectual or psychological appeal, but from a moral or ethical standpoint, they could be damaging.

Even if someone is not very Godly—or even nice—the Divine soul is an indelible part of the person. You cannot eradicate it. You *can* cause it to go into hibernation, though. If your life is filled with wrong-headed ideas and actions, your Divine soul will go to sleep because it becomes lonely and isolated. It has no one to talk to. This might explain why people who are active achievers can still feel unfulfilled and experience ennui. Their animal soul is doing fine, as animals go, but their Divine soul feels isolated in the middle of the animal soul's partying.

Can we lead our egos and animalistic drives toward a path that is far Godlier than its crude nature would suggest? Yes. In fact, our mission as developed human beings is to educate the intellectual drive to bring the Divine and animal souls into harmony. With this spiritual GPS, we can harmonize and integrate the Divine soul, the animal soul, and the intellectual drive. We want them to speak to one another and block any evil ideas from getting a word in edgewise. Once these three forces are in harmony, the Divine soul can work on the animal soul to channel itself into appropriate—even holy—pursuits.

Why is this balance important? Crisis, tragedy, and suffering can throw us off balance completely. During emotionally fragile times, many people will default and allow the animal soul to take charge. This can happen in any number of ways. People who become depressed may go into hibernation. They may act out in ways that temporarily numb or distract from the pain but damage the body and the spirit, such as overeating or undereating, drinking to excess or abusing drugs, or engaging in inappropriate relationships. At such a vulnerable time, even the mind will conspire with the animal drive in search of the next soothing release or indulgence, rather than steering the person toward a more psychologically healthy, morally correct path.

To prevent pain and panic from taking over, reharmonize your soul's drives

How easy it is to fall into such an emotional and intellectual imbalance. Grief and suffering tend to make a person myopic, their world much smaller, so this negative path is a dangerous, slippery slope. Once you recognize that this has happened, it's vital to take small, steady steps to reharmonize your dual souls and your intellectual drive. This is the key to helping you work through your suffering. By maintaining a balance between the Divine soul, the animal soul, and the intellectual drive, you prevent your world from shrinking to only your pain or your panic. Instead, you can keep your world open, perhaps even expand it.

One of the most effective ways to keep your world open in the face of suffering is to resist the temptation to simply hold on tight and just exist. Instead, choosing life is choosing to *act*. Rabbi Lord Jonathan Sacks used the example of Abraham, *old and advanced in years*, who limited the time he sat and grieved and dwelled on his sadness after the loss of his beloved wife, Sarah.

> *His grief is described in a mere five Hebrew words: in English, "Abraham came to mourn for Sarah and to weep for her." Then immediately we read, "And Abraham rose from his grief."[11] From then on, he engaged in a flurry of activity with two aims in mind: first to buy a plot of land in which to bury Sarah, second to find a wife for his son.... Abraham did not wait for God to act. He understood one of the profoundest truths of Judaism: that God is waiting for us to act.[12]*

How did Abraham overcome the trauma and the grief? How do you survive almost losing your child—his son Isaac—and actually losing your life partner—Sarah—and still summon the will to keep going? What gave Abraham his resilience, his ability to survive, with his spirit intact?

> *Rabbi Sacks wrote:*

> *I learned the answer from the people who became my mentors in moral courage, namely the Holocaust survivors I had the privilege to know.... The survivors I knew had the most tenacious hold on life. I wanted to understand how they kept going....*

> *Eventually I discovered [how]. Most of them did not talk about the past, even to their marriage partners, even to their children. Instead, they set about creating a new life in a new land. They learned its language and customs. They found work. They built careers. They married and had children. Having lost their own families, the survivors became an extended family to one another. They looked forward, not back. First, they built a future.*

*Only then—sometimes forty or fifty years later—did
they speak about the past. That was when they told their
story, first to their families, then to the world.*[13] *First
you have to build a future. Only then can you mourn the
past.*

*God enters our lives as a call from the future. It is as
if we hear Him beckoning to us from the far horizon
of time, urging us to take a journey and undertake a
task that, in ways we cannot fully understand, we were
created for... .*

*We are not here by accident. We are here because God
wanted us to be, and because there is a task we were
meant to fulfill.*[14]

Jews are a people of optimism—otherwise, how could
we have survived our history? But you don't have to be
Jewish to choose to look ahead to a brighter tomorrow.
This is not only possible but even probable if you summon
your internal strength right now.

Wouldn't it be nice if we could all live our lives in tranquility and prosperity, with the people we love passing
away peacefully in their sleep after nine decades of a rich,
fulfilling life? We who are left behind hope we will merit this same blessed transition. But that isn't the world
God made for us. Our world includes rude shocks, ruined
opportunities, disappointments, failures, and untimely
deaths. How well we handle these roadblocks and sor-
rows depends largely on approaching life with maturity
and an eye toward the future—like adults, not children.

We need the right role models and teachers to learn
how to adopt this mature and forward-facing mindset. In
Jewish tradition, we begin with the sacred texts. We also

look to the people we know who are continuing to grow in spirit while making the right ethical decisions. These should be our teachers.

Rabbi Sacks asserts that each of us has a task to fulfill, even if we don't fully understand it. The Torah makes this clear almost immediately as one after another individual is sent out to fulfill their role in the destiny of the Jewish people: Abraham, Rebecca, Moses, Joshua, David, Solomon, the Prophets, Ruth, Esther, and many others.

A while after my wife passed away, I poured out my heart in a letter to my Rebbe, guide, and mentor, the Lubavitcher Rebbe, Rabbi Menachem Mendel Schneerson. He responded to me personally, writing: "When God gives someone a mission—and we all have a mission—He gives the person the strength not only to fulfill it but to do it with joy, and of 'good heart' [i.e., good attitude]." That's what our forebears did, and that is what God wants of us and empowers us to do.

As King Solomon advised, *Go, eat your bread in gladness and drink your wine in joy, for your action was long ago approved by God.... Whatever it is in your power to do with your might, do it.*[15]

Study and learn. Listen to good counsel and speak out against evil. Care for yourself and others. Learn to become a living example of faith and strength.

Comfort, and be comforted.

Chapter Summary: *The suffering that God allows will always remain beyond our understanding in this physical lifetime, but we can take comfort that the soul lives on eternally, on a higher plane,* *having completed its earthly mission. In our lives we can work to harmonize our Divine and animal souls and our intellect, so that we can come closer to achieving the mission that God has sent us here to fulfill. And we need to resist remaining stuck in paralyzing grief; instead, becoming future-focused—knowing that life is meant to be lived.*

Endnotes:

1   *Avot* 2:4.
2   Exodus 23:3.
3   *Mechilta, Shemot* 15.
4   Exodus 20:15.
5   Richard G. Tedeschi and Lawrence G. Calhoun, "The Posttraumatic Growth Inventory: Measuring the Positive Legacy of Trauma," *Journal of Traumatic Stress,* Vol. 9, #3, 1996.
6   Leviticus 25:35.
7   This is part of the "Hierarchy of Needs" theory, first introduced by Abraham H. Maslow in "A Theory of Human Motivation," *Psychological Review,* Vol. 50, #4, 1943.
8   Proverbs 17:17.
9   *Shemot Rabbah* 27:1.
10 *Kaddish* by Leon Wieseltier, former literary editor of *The New Republic*; and *Living a Year of Kaddish*, by Ari L. Goldman, professor of Journalism at Columbia University and a former reporter for *The New York Times*.
11 Genesis 23:2–3.
12 Rabbi Lord Jonathan Sacks, "Covenant & Conversation: A Call from the Future, Chayei Sarah 5776," rabbisacks.org.
13 Ibid.
14 Ibid.
15 Ecclesiastes 9:7, 10.

Adversity Doesn't Define Us. How We Respond to it Does.

My book ends, and I want to leave you with some parting thoughts.

It is up to us to make our losses matter. I believe that whatever happens to us isn't just arbitrary. They happen for a reason and a purpose. The reason might elude us, but the purpose is clear: for us to seek and then absorb the lessons we might take from our experiences. It is up to us to make sense of our losses and become better from them, to grow because of them.

If you are in pain, don't run away from it. Stay with it. Let it wash over you like a wave. You will survive, you will be stronger, and you will be able to deal with the next wave with added stamina. If you don't yet have the courage to face it on your own, do it with a friend or with a trained counselor, in a safe and supportive environment.

I recognize that there is no single recipe to cope with and overcome life's painful challenges and losses. Some feel shame in their unaccustomed state of "weakness."

Others need time to catch their breath from the traumatic blow they have experienced. But know this: God is confident that you can and will survive, and by taking charge and working things through, you will actually thrive. God didn't bring you this challenge so that you should merely survive. He wants you to grow: to become better, stronger, and more resilient because of it.

Find your inner reserve. There's more to you than you realize—even physically. There was a British newspaper story about two women, aged twenty-four and twenty-nine, headlined "'Supermothers' and Grandfather Lift One-Ton Renault Clio off Trapped Schoolboy,"[1] a feat totally beyond their abilities until they needed to save the boy. They accessed a reserve of physical strength that macho bodybuilders wish they had. Like a car struggling to climb a steep grade, in times of extreme need, we shift our transmission into a lower gear and, *voilà*, we get better traction and thrust, and we keep going, even stronger than before. Emotionally, we can also access our resilience to keep going, even using our pain to turbocharge us forward.

It has been said many times, but it bears repeating because it is so true: Attitude is everything. We are not victims to whom a tragedy "happened." Each of us is the captain of our ship and master of our destiny. But after we are thrown a curve ball, can we still hit it out of the park? During Viktor Frankl's hell on earth as a death camp inmate, he experienced the most unimaginable atrocities a human being could suffer. He saw his parents, wife, and brothers perish before his eyes. Of their family, only he and his sister survived.

One day, when Frankl was left naked and alone in a small room, he started to become aware of what he famously identified as "the last of the human freedoms." The Nazi captors could take away his physical freedom, but they could not take away his freedom of identity. Frankl was the only one capable of deciding how those atrocities were going to affect him. The result of these harrowing yet life-changing experiences became the source of his classic book, *Man's Search for Meaning.*

Adversity doesn't define us. How we respond to it does.

If you are in pain, be it physical, emotional, or psychic, take the opportunity to focus on others who are also in pain. Is it possible that you may not have paid attention to their distress or pain? By reaching out to another, you will both be helping each other.

Seeing yourself as a victim of circumstances is self-fulfilling. If this is the message you repeat to yourself, *you will become a victim.* But you can turn this on its head and instead see yourself as a person who has been purposefully challenged to prove your mettle. This internal message will bring forth your resilience and strength.

We have to start new every day, and sometimes, many times a day

God is the architect of your struggle. God—the Celestial Potter—will not give you a burden greater than you can handle, even if, at first, you're not so sure about how much strength you truly have inside. God gives us opportunities for growth. Just as exercising the body makes muscles grow (a process called hypertrophy), and exercising the brain makes the brain cells grow (a process called neuroplasticity), so, too, we have built-in coping mechanisms for emotional and spiritual growth.

But it is up to us to consciously submit to our trials, knowing they were sent by our Creator, God. It is up to us to accept that this is an intended event, whether or not we understand it, appreciate it, and feel ready to meet the challenge. We need to embrace the mindset that, somehow, this is for our benefit.

When the surf is high, it can be dangerous for the uninitiated. The strength of the waves can knock you down, drag you under, and knock you out by its kinetic force. An experienced surfer knows how to time the waves and dive right into and under the wave as it approaches, then swim out behind the wave, get on top of it, and ride it in to shore with great exhilaration.

Life's waves come at us inexorably, sometimes gently and pleasantly, sometimes surging powerfully, seemingly threatening to overwhelm us. Don't fight the waves. Know that you can ride the wave by diving into its core and recognizing that there's a positive plan in what appears to be destructive. If you commit to learning to do this, you can have an exhilarating, positive, life-expanding growth experience. As Nietzsche said, "What does not kill me makes me stronger."[2]

The pain of losing our loved ones, especially in tragic circumstances, may recede, but it will always be there. That's okay. Just know that the soul of your loved one now lives on a higher plane and continues to care about us as we do for them. They benefit from the good deeds done on their behalf.

Rabbi Nachman of Breslov said, "We have to start new every day, and sometimes, many times a day." Sometimes we just have to take a deep breath and start again.

Comfort and be comforted. God cares about your loss more than you realize. And although we haven't met, so do I.

Endnotes:

1   *Daily Mail*, June 4, 2009.
2   Friedrich Nietzsche, *Twilight of the Idols* (1888).

Acknowledgments

I give thanks to You, Lord, our God, King of the universe, Who has granted me life and health, and Who has sustained me and enabled me to reach this occasion.

In writing this book, I've benefited from the editorial help and emotional support of many friends and other fine people, who became friends in the process, whom I want to acknowledge.

Jay Litvin, though long gone from this earthly abode, reviewed and commented on my early manuscript and encouraged me to continue with the project, which I heeded because he was who he was. Without Michael Levin this book would not have gotten off the ground. Without Judy Gruen it would not have had the smooth landing that it did.

During the interim, many have stepped in to keep the project aloft. Harold Glicken, who heard me out and encouraged me when I didn't know what I was doing; Rishe Deitsch, who has been a friend for half a century and my go-to editor for over twenty-five years; Sterna Citron, for making herself available for editorial help consistently and graciously; Ya'akovah Weber, who did much more than proofreading; and Rabbi Chaim Citron, with whom I reviewed the philosophical and theological issues in the book and who provided invaluable advice.

Special appreciation goes to my wife, Chana Rachel, who, in addition to her insightful editing and critique, put up with me with the patience only a wise and capacious spirit could and would, and did.

While I'm indebted to each of those mentioned for their positive contributions, responsibility for any flaws and errors are mine only.

תושלב"ע